Make the most of EGGS

22/11/1996.

A nice change from "...lettes"!

We have all heard the saying 'If there is an egg in the house there's a meal in the house'. Eggs are one of nature's fast foods – it takes only minutes to whisk up and cook an omelette or to create delicious pancakes. For something that's sure to impress, a light soufflé – whether it's sweet or savoury – must be your choice everytime.

This book presents a wonderful collection of dishes that use eggs as their main ingredient. You will find recipes for imaginative breakfasts and brunches, inspiring main meals and tempting desserts.

THE PANTRY SHELF

Unless otherwise stated, the following ingredients used in this book are:

Cream   Double, suitable for whipping
Flour   White flour, plain or standard
Sugar   White sugar

WHAT'S IN A TABLESPOON?

NEW ZEALAND
1 tablespoon =
15 mL OR 3 teaspoons
UNITED KINGDOM
1 tablespoon =
15 mL OR 3 teaspoons
AUSTRALIA
1 tablespoon =
20 mL OR 4 teaspoons
The recipes in this book were tested in Australia where a 20 mL tablespoon is standard. All measures are level.

The tablespoon in the New Zealand and United Kingdom sets of measuring spoons is 15 mL. In many recipes this difference will not matter. For recipes using baking powder, gelatine, bicarbonate of soda, small quantities of flour and cornflour, simply add another teaspoon for each tablespoon specified.

CONTENTS

BREAKFASTS

*An egg for breakfast is a wonderful way to start the day.
While the following recipes are a little more elaborate than you
would make on a day-to-day basis, they are just perfect for that
special weekend breakfast or brunch.*

Blueberry Pancakes

Eggs Benedict

Pipérade

Egg and Avocado
Tomatoes

Savoury Scramblers

Banana Pancakes

Blueberry Pancakes

2

BLUEBERRY PANCAKES

1 cup/170 g/5^{1}/$_2$ oz corn meal (polenta)
1 cup/125 g/4 oz self-raising flour, sifted
1 teaspoon bicarbonate of soda
2 tablespoons golden syrup
60 g/2 oz butter, melted
2 cups/500 mL/16 fl oz buttermilk
or milk
1 egg, beaten
250 g/8 oz fresh or frozen blueberries

RASPBERRY SAUCE
250 g/8 oz fresh or frozen raspberries
2 tablespoons golden syrup

Makes 24 pancakes

1   Place corn meal (polenta), self-raising flour and bicarbonate of soda in a bowl and mix to combine. Make a well in the centre of the flour mixture and add golden syrup, butter, buttermilk or milk and egg. Mix well to combine. Stir in blueberries.

2   Heat a lightly greased frying pan over a medium heat. When pan is hot, add 3 tablespoons of pancake mixture and cook for 2-3 minutes each side or until lightly browned. Remove pancake from pan and keep warm. Repeat with remaining mixture.

3   To make sauce, place raspberries and golden syrup in a food processor or blender and process to make a purée. Push mixture through a sieve, place in a small saucepan and cook over a medium heat for 3-4 minutes or until sauce is warm. Serve sauce spooned over pancakes.

Serve these pancakes with fresh juice for a special breakfast or brunch. They also make a delicious dessert.
The pancakes can be made ahead of time and frozen if you wish. When you are ready to serve them, simply reheat, covered, in a low oven or in the microwave.

EGGS BENEDICT

2 teaspoons olive oil
4 spring onions, chopped
1 green pepper, cut into strips
3 slices ham, chopped
4 eggs
2 English muffins, split and toasted

HOLLANDAISE SAUCE
3 egg yolks
3 tablespoons water
^{1}/$_4$ teaspoon cayenne pepper
185 g/6 oz butter, clarified
1 tablespoon lemon juice

1   Heat oil in a frying pan and cook spring onions and green pepper for 3-4 minutes or until soft. Stir in ham and set aside.

2   Break eggs into lightly greased egg poacher cups and poach in 2.5 cm/1 in boiling water for 4-5 minutes or until whites are firm.

3   To make sauce, place egg yolks, water and cayenne pepper in a bowl and whisk until light in colour. Place bowl over a saucepan of simmering water and cook, whisking constantly, until mixture thickens. Remove saucepan from heat and whisk in butter a little at a time. Stir in lemon juice and set sauce aside to cool for 5 minutes.

4   Top each muffin with a little ham mixture, a cooked egg and a little sauce.

Serves 4

The process of clarifying butter separates it into three layers: a top layer of foam, a middle layer of pure butterfat and a bottom layer of milky-white solids. It is the middle layer that is used for sautéing; the other two layers contain water, milk proteins and carbohydrates.
To clarify butter, place it in a small saucepan and melt it over a low heat. Skim the foam from the surface of the butter, then slowly pour the butter into a bowl, leaving behind the milky-white solids. Ghee, which is used in Indian cooking, is a type of clarified butter.

PIPERADE

8 eggs
¹/₂ cup/125 mL/4 fl oz orange juice
¹/₃ cup/90 mL/3 fl oz cream (double)
30 g/1 oz butter

PIPERADE
30 g/1 oz butter
1 small leek, sliced
250 g/8 oz ham, diced
1 teaspoon dried oregano
1 green pepper, chopped
1 yellow or red pepper, chopped
125 g/4 oz cherry tomatoes, halved
freshly ground black pepper

1   To make Pipérade, melt butter in a frying pan and cook leek, ham, oregano, green and yellow or red peppers for 4-5 minutes or until leek and peppers are soft. Add tomatoes and cook for 2-3 minutes or until tomatoes are heated. Season to taste with black pepper. Set aside and keep warm.

2   Place eggs, orange juice, cream and black pepper to taste in a bowl and mix to combine. Melt butter in a frying pan, add egg mixture and cook over a low heat. As the egg mixture starts to set, gently turn it, so that the mixture forms large fluffy rolls – do not use a stirring motion as this causes the rolls to break up. Cook until all the egg mixture is just set.

3   Spoon egg around the outside of a large serving platter, then spoon vegetable mixture into the centre.

Serves 8

Served with hot toast this is a substantial breakfast or brunch dish. You will also find it makes an excellent lunch or dinner dish.

EGG AND AVOCADO TOMATOES

Above: Pipérade
Left: Egg and Avocado Tomatoes

4 large tomatoes
4 eggs, lightly beaten
1 tablespoon snipped fresh chives
¹/4 avocado, peeled and chopped
freshly ground black pepper
60 g/2 oz butter
4 teaspoons sour cream
or natural yogurt

1   Cut tops from tomatoes and scoop out seeds and flesh to make tomato shells.

2   Place eggs, chives, avocado and black pepper to taste in a bowl and mix to combine. Melt butter in a frying pan over a low heat, add egg mixture and cook, stirring gently, until set but still creamy.

3   Divide egg mixture between tomato shells and top each egg-filled tomato with a teaspoon of sour cream or yogurt.

Serves 4

A wonderful combination of flavours, these tomatoes are just right for that special breakfast, brunch or supper.

SAVOURY SCRAMBLERS

Scrambled eggs cook well in the microwave. To cook in the microwave, prepare egg mixture as described in recipe. Melt butter in a microwave-safe jug or dish and cook on HIGH (100%) for 20 seconds or until melted. Add egg mixture and cook on HIGH (100%) for 5 minutes, or until egg mixture is set but still creamy. Stir twice during cooking.

8 eggs
2 tablespoons milk
freshly ground black pepper
15 g/^{1}/$_2$ oz butter

1 Place eggs and milk in a bowl and using a whisk, beat to combine. Season to taste with black pepper.

2 Melt butter over a low heat in a medium, heavy-based saucepan. Add egg mixture and cook, stirring gently, until the egg mixture is set but still creamy. Serve immediately.

Serves 4

Savoury Scramblers

BANANA PANCAKES

Banana Pancakes

1 cup/155 g/5 oz wholemeal flour, sifted
and husks returned
1¼ cups/315 mL/10 fl oz milk
1 egg, lightly beaten
2 teaspoons honey
1 teaspoon oil

BANANA FILLING
2 tablespoons chopped raisins
1 tablespoon water
2 tablespoons honey
1 teaspoon lemon juice
2 bananas, sliced

STRAWBERRY SAUCE
250 g/8 oz strawberries
2 teaspoons lemon juice

Serves 6

1 Place flour in a bowl and gradually stir in milk, egg and honey. Beat mixture until smooth, then stir in oil. Heat a lightly greased frying pan over a medium heat. When hot, add 3 tablespoons of pancake mixture and cook for 2-3 minutes each side or until lightly browned. Remove pancake from pan and repeat with remaining mixture.

2 To make filling, place raisins in a bowl, add water and set aside to soak for 15 minutes. Stir in honey and lemon juice. Place bananas in a bowl and mix in honey mixture. Spoon a small amount of banana mixture onto each pancake and fold. Place pancakes in a single layer in an ovenproof dish, cover and bake for 10 minutes or until heated through.

3 To make sauce, place strawberries and lemon juice in a food processor or blender and process until smooth. Push sauce through a sieve and spoon over pancakes.

Oven temperature
180°C, 350°F, Gas 4

Pancakes are cooked on the first side when little bubbles appear on the top of the pancake. Flip and cook the other side until lightly browned.

QUICK MEALS

*Whether you need a speedy lunch or a hasty dinner,
eggs are sure to fit the bill. Packed with goodness and taste,
the egg recipes in this section can be prepared and cooked
in next to no time.*

Vegetable Frittata

VEGETABLE FRITTATA

3 tablespoons olive oil
1 onion, sliced
10 asparagus spears, trimmed and cut
into 2.5 cm/1 in pieces
2 zucchini (courgettes), cut
into thin strips
1 red pepper, cut into thin strips
8 eggs, lightly beaten
4 tablespoons grated Parmesan cheese
3 tablespoons sour cream
or natural yogurt
freshly ground black pepper

1   Heat oil in a large frying pan and cook onion, asparagus, zucchini (courgettes) and red pepper over a medium heat for 3-4 minutes or until vegetables just start to soften.

2   Place eggs, Parmesan cheese, sour cream or yogurt and black pepper to taste in a bowl and beat to combine. Pour egg mixture over vegetables in pan, reduce heat to low and cook for 10 minutes or until frittata is almost set.

3   Place frying pan under a preheated medium grill and cook frittata for 2-3 minutes or until top is set. Serve cut into wedges.

Serves 4

For a complete meal, serve this frittata with a salad of lettuce, mushrooms and mandarin segments tossed in a garlicky vinaigrette dressing.

EGG AND SPRING ONION SPIRALS

1 loaf unsliced wholemeal bread
125 g/4 oz butter, softened
8 hard-boiled eggs
2 tablespoons mayonnaise
2 tablespoons sour cream or
natural yogurt
4 spring onions, finely chopped
$1/2$ teaspoon dry mustard
freshly ground black pepper

1   Trim crusts from bread and cut loaf into 8 slices lengthwise. Spread one side of each slice lightly with butter.

2   Place eggs, mayonnaise, sour cream or yogurt, spring onions, mustard and black pepper to taste in a bowl and mash to combine. Divide egg mixture between bread slices and spread to cover each slice.

3   Place egg-covered bread slices on plastic food wrap and roll up, using wrap as a guide. Refrigerate until ready to use, then slice into rounds.

Makes 48 slices

Did you know? The colour of the egg yolk is affected by what the hen eats, but no matter what the colour the nutritional value of the yolk remains the same.

FRENCH OMELETTE

2 eggs
1 tablespoon cold water
freshly ground black pepper
15 g/^{1}/$_2$ oz butter

For best results, prepare and cook omelettes quickly and serve immediately. Remember, if the heat is too high, or the omelette is cooked for too long, it will be tough and dry. Try one of these delicious fillings or make your own favourite combinations.

1 Place eggs, water and black pepper to taste in a bowl and whisk lightly to combine.

Serves 1

2 Heat an omelette pan over a medium heat until hot. Add butter, tipping the pan so the base is completely coated. Heat until the butter is foaming, but not browned, then add the egg mixture. As it sets use a palette knife or fork to gently draw up the edge of the omelette until no liquid remains and the omelette is lightly set.

3 Serve omelette plain, or topped with filling of your choice, and fold in half. Slip omelette onto a plate and serve immediately.

AVOCADO AND BACON FILLING

1 tablespoon sour cream
or natural yogurt
1 teaspoon snipped fresh chives
^{1}/$_2$ teaspoon French mustard
1 rasher bacon, chopped
^{1}/$_4$ avocado, stoned, peeled and chopped

1 Place sour cream or yogurt, chives and mustard in a bowl and mix to combine. Cook bacon in a small frying pan for 2-3 minutes or until crisp. Remove and drain on absorbent kitchen paper.

2 Spread sour cream or yogurt mixture over one half of an omelette and top with bacon and avocado. Fold omelette and serve immediately.

VEGETARIAN FILLING

1 teaspoon olive oil
1 tablespoon chopped green pepper
1 tablespoon finely chopped onion
1 small clove garlic, crushed
^{1}/$_2$ tomato, peeled and chopped
1 black olive, sliced
1 teaspoon finely chopped fresh basil
freshly ground black pepper

The simplest of all fillings for an omelette is freshly chopped herbs, either a single herb or a mixture. Herbs that are delicious with eggs include basil, parsley, chives, dill, mint, thyme and marjoram.

1 Heat oil in a small frying pan and cook green pepper, onion and garlic over a medium heat for 2-3 minutes or until onion is soft. Add tomato, olive and basil and cook for 5 minutes longer. Season to taste with black pepper.

2 Place filling on one half of an omelette, fold and serve immediately.

French Omelette with Avocado and Bacon Filling, and Vegetarian Filling

QUAIL EGG SALAD

12 quails' eggs
1 tablespoon olive oil
2 cloves garlic, crushed
2 leeks, cut into thin strips
1 radicchio, leaves separated and washed
or ¼ finely shredded red cabbage

FRENCH DRESSING
1 clove garlic, crushed
2 tablespoons olive oil
3 tablespoons lemon juice
freshly ground black pepper

1 Bring a large saucepan of water to the boil, add quails' eggs and cook for 3 minutes. Drain and set aside to cool. Shell eggs and reserve.

2 Heat oil in a large frying pan over a medium heat and cook garlic and leeks for 3 minutes or until tender. Arrange radicchio leaves or red cabbage on four plates, top with warm leek mixture and three eggs.

3 To make dressing, place garlic, oil, lemon juice and black pepper to taste in a screwtop jar and shake to combine. Sprinkle dressing over salads and serve immediately.

Serves 4

If quails' eggs are unavailable, this salad is just as delicious made with hens' eggs. Use 3 hens' eggs, hard-boiled and cut into quarters, in place of the quails' eggs.

Left: Spring Omelette
Far Left: Quail Egg Salad

SPRING OMELETTE

15 g/^{1}/$_2$ oz butter
4 eggs, lightly beaten
3 tablespoons milk
freshly ground black pepper
3 tablespoons grated tasty cheese
(mature Cheddar)

VEGETABLE FILLING
15 g/^{1}/$_2$ oz butter
2 spring onions, finely chopped
6 button mushrooms, sliced
^{1}/$_2$ small red pepper, cut into thin strips
1 teaspoon chopped fresh coriander

1   To make filling, melt butter in a frying pan and cook spring onions, mushrooms, red pepper and coriander for 2 minutes or until vegetables are tender. Remove vegetables from pan, set aside and keep warm.

2   Melt butter in a clean frying pan. Place eggs, milk and black pepper to taste in a bowl and whisk to combine. Pour egg mixture into pan and, as the omelette cooks, use a palette knife or fork to gently draw up the edge of the omelette until no liquid remains and the omelette is lightly set. Top half the omelette with filling, then sprinkle with cheese. Fold omelette over, cut in half, slide onto serving plates and serve immediately.

Serves 2

For a quick and nutritious meal, serve this omelette with crusty rolls and finish with a piece of fruit.

13

FRENCH ONION FLANS

Oven temperature
200°C, 400°F, Gas 6

Individual flans are delicious
eaten hot, warm or cold.
They can be made in
advance and frozen, to
have on hand for a quick
meal. Allow to thaw, then
reheat at 180°C/350°F/Gas 4
for 10-15 minutes or until
heated through.

250 g/8 oz prepared puff pastry
170 g/5^1/$_2$ oz grated tasty cheese
(mature Cheddar)

ONION FILLING
60 g/2 oz butter
6 onions, sliced
3 eggs
1^3/$_4$ cups/350 g/11 oz sour cream
or natural yogurt
1 teaspoon ground nutmeg
1^1/$_2$ teaspoons horseradish relish

1 Roll out pastry and use to line six
lightly greased 10 cm/4 in flan tins.

2 To make filling, melt butter in a frying
pan and cook onions over a low heat for
10-15 minutes or until golden. Divide
into six portions and spread over base of
flans.

3 Place eggs, sour cream or yogurt,
nutmeg and horseradish in a bowl and
mix to combine. Pour egg mixture into
flans and sprinkle with grated cheese.
Bake for 20 minutes or until flans are set.

Serves 6

ASPARAGUS WITH DILL HOLLANDAISE

500 g/1 lb asparagus, trimmed

DILL HOLLANDAISE SAUCE
3 egg yolks
1 tablespoon lemon juice
125 g/4 oz butter
1 tablespoon chopped fresh dill
freshly ground black pepper

1 Boil, steam or microwave asparagus
until just tender. Drain, set aside and
keep warm.

2 To make hollandaise sauce, place egg
yolks and lemon juice in a food processor
or blender and process until light and
fluffy. Melt butter until it is hot and
bubbling. With food processor running,
slowly pour in melted butter and process
until sauce is thick. Stir in dill and season
to taste with black pepper. Spoon sauce
over asparagus and serve immediately.

Serves 4

If dill is unavailable you might
like to make this hollandaise
sauce using parsley or chives,
or simply leave it plain.

*French Onion Flans,
Asparagus with Dill Hollandaise*

ASPARAGUS OMELETTE

2 eggs
1 tablespoon water
freshly ground black pepper
15 g/¹/₂ oz butter
3 canned asparagus spears, drained,
or 3 fresh asparagus spears, trimmed
and cooked until tender

Serves 1

1 Place eggs, water and black pepper to taste in a bowl and whisk to combine.

2 Melt butter in an omelette pan over a medium heat. Add egg mixture to pan and cook, continually drawing the edge of the omelette in with a fork until no liquid remains and the omelette is lightly set.

3 Place asparagus spears in centre of omelette, fold omelette and slide onto a plate. Serve immediately.

This omelette is also delicious filled with sliced canned artichoke hearts.

PROVENCAL EGGS

¹/₂ cup/125 mL/4 fl oz vegetable oil
1 large onion, chopped
2 cloves garlic, crushed
1 eggplant (aubergine), chopped
4 large tomatoes, chopped
3 tablespoons tomato paste (purée)
¹/₄ cup/60 mL/2 fl oz white wine
4 eggs
1 tablespoon chopped fresh parsley

1   Heat 2 tablespoons oil in a large frying pan and cook onion and garlic for 3-4 minutes or until onion is soft.

2   Add eggplant (aubergine) and remaining oil and cook for 5 minutes. Stir in tomatoes, tomato paste (purée) and wine and cook for 10 minutes longer. Transfer vegetable mixture to a shallow ovenproof dish and bake for 10 minutes.

3   Remove dish from oven and using the back of a tablespoon make four depressions in the vegetable mixture. Break an egg into each depression, sprinkle with parsley and bake for 10-15 minutes longer or until eggs are cooked.

Serves 4

These eggs can also be cooked in shallow individual dishes. Divide the vegetable mixture between the dishes, bake for 5 minutes then add the eggs and bake for 10 minutes longer or until eggs are cooked. Served in individual dishes this is a delightful brunch or supper dish.

Below: Cheesy Baked Eggs
Bottom Left: Provençal Eggs

CHEESY BAKED EGGS

30 g/1 oz butter
250 g/8 oz mushrooms, chopped
1 lettuce, shredded
1 tablespoon Worcestershire sauce
freshly ground black pepper
4 eggs
60 g/2 oz grated tasty cheese
(mature Cheddar)

1   Melt butter in a frying pan and cook mushrooms and lettuce, stirring, for 4-5 minutes or until mushrooms are tender. Stir in Worcestershire sauce and season to taste with black pepper. Divide mushroom mixture between four 1 cup/250 mL/ 8 fl oz capacity ovenproof ramekins.

2   Break an egg into each ramekin and sprinkle with cheese. Bake for 10-15 minutes or until eggs are cooked and cheese is melted.

Serves 4

Oven temperature
200°C, 400°F, Gas 6

It is best to bring eggs to room temperature before using. Remove the eggs from the refrigerator 30 minutes before use or run them under warm water for a short time. Eggs at room temperature cook more evenly and if you are beating them they will have an increased volume.

MAIN MEALS

*As an alternative to meat, chicken or seafood, eggs
make a great main meal. Whether you serve a Corn and Chilli
Soufflé, a Leek and Apple Pie or a Spinach Pancake Stack,
you can be sure that dinner will be a hit.*

Scotch Eggs

18

SCOTCH EGGS

500 g/1 lb sausage meat
4 hard-boiled eggs, shelled
1 egg
pinch cayenne pepper
1 cup/125 g/4 oz dried bread crumbs
oil for deep-frying

1   Divide sausage meat into four portions and, using damp hands, mould a portion around each hard-boiled egg to completely enclose it.

2   Place egg and cayenne pepper in a bowl and whisk to combine. Dip each sausage-wrapped egg in egg mixture and roll in bread crumbs. Place prepared eggs on a plate lined with plastic food wrap, cover and refrigerate for 15-20 minutes.

3   Heat oil in a large deep saucepan and cook prepared eggs for 7-10 minutes or until golden. Drain on absorbent kitchen paper and serve immediately.

Serves 4

Scotch Eggs are a popular lunch box treat. For something a little different you might like to use a mixture of mashed potato and canned salmon flavoured with herbs in place of the sausage meat. To coat 4 eggs you will need 200 g/6^{1}/2 oz canned pink or red salmon, 2 potatoes, cooked and mashed, 1 tablespoon snipped fresh chives and 1 tablespoon finely chopped fresh parsley. Place all ingredients in a bowl and mix to combine. Use as described in recipe.

POTATO AND EGG PIES

1 kg/2 lb prepared puff pastry
1 egg, lightly beaten

POTATO AND LEEK FILLING
30 g/1 oz butter
4 leeks, sliced
2 cloves garlic, crushed
2 teaspoons curry powder
6 potatoes, peeled and cooked until just tender
4 hard-boiled eggs, chopped
2 x 350 g/11 oz canned asparagus cuts (tips) or canned peas, drained
3 tablespoons chopped fresh parsley
^{2}/3 cup/170 g/5^{1}/2 oz sour cream
2 egg yolks, lightly beaten
125 g/4 oz grated tasty cheese (mature Cheddar)
freshly ground black pepper
1 egg, lightly beaten
caraway seeds

Makes 8 individual pies

1   To make filling, melt butter in a frying pan and cook leeks over a medium heat for 2-3 minutes or until soft. Stir in garlic and curry powder and cook for 1 minute longer. Remove pan from heat.

2   Chop potatoes and place in a bowl with leek mixture, chopped eggs, asparagus or peas, parsley, sour cream, egg yolks, cheese and black pepper to taste. Mix to combine and set aside to cool.

3   Roll out pastry and use two-thirds to line base and sides of eight greased metal pie dishes. Cut remaining pastry to fit top of pies. Spoon filling into pie dishes, brush pastry edges with egg and top with pie lids. Press edges together to seal. Make a slit in the top of each pie using a sharp knife. Brush tops of pies with beaten egg, sprinkle with caraway seeds and bake for 15 minutes. Reduce oven temperature to 180°C/350°F/Gas 4 and bake for 15 minutes or until golden brown.

Oven temperature
220°C, 425°F, Gas 7

For a complete meal, serve these pies hot, warm or at room temperature accompanied by a crisp green salad. Leftover pies make ideal lunch box or picnic fare.

CHEESE ROULADE

2 zucchini (courgettes), grated
4 eggs, separated
2 tablespoons grated Gruyère cheese
3 tablespoons grated Parmesan cheese
$1/2$ teaspoon ground nutmeg
freshly ground black pepper

CHEESE FILLING
30 g/1 oz butter
$1/4$ cup/30 g/1 oz flour
$1^1/4$ cups/315 mL/10 fl oz milk
185 g/6 oz ricotta or full-fat soft cheese,
drained

1   To make filling, melt butter in a saucepan over a medium heat and cook flour for 1 minute. Remove pan from heat and stir in milk. Return pan to a low heat and cook, stirring, for 4-5 minutes or until sauce boils and thickens. Remove 2 tablespoons of sauce and set aside to use for the roulade. Stir ricotta or full-fat soft cheese into remaining sauce and set aside.

2   Cook zucchini (courgettes) in 2 tablespoons of water or in the microwave until soft. Drain and pat dry using absorbent kitchen paper. Place zucchini (courgettes), reserved 2 tablespoons sauce, egg yolks, Gruyère cheese, Parmesan cheese, nutmeg and black pepper to taste in a bowl and mix to combine.

3   Place egg whites in a clean bowl and beat until stiff peaks form. Fold egg white mixture into zucchini (courgette) mixture. Spoon into a greased and lined 25 x 30 cm/10 x 12 in Swiss roll tin and bake for 12-15 minutes or until roulade is set. Turn roulade onto a wire rack covered with a clean teatowel and, while still warm, roll up from short end, Swiss roll style. Hold for 30 seconds then unroll. Carefully remove paper and teatowel and set aside to cool for 5 minutes. Spread filling evenly over roulade and roll up again. Serve at room temperature.

An elegant luncheon dish, this roulade makes entertaining easy and is sure to impress. It can be made several hours ahead of time and is delicious served with a julienne of vegetables.

Serves 6

*'One of the easiest ways to separate eggs is to give the shell a sharp
tap with a knife and then to allow the white to drain
slowly through the hole.'*

Corn and Chilli Soufflé

CORN AND CHILLI SOUFFLE

3 tablespoons bread crumbs, made
from stale bread
60 g/2 oz butter
1 onion, finely chopped
1 red chilli, seeds removed and
finely chopped
$^1/_4$ cup/30 g/1 oz flour
$^1/_2$ cup/125 mL/4 fl oz milk
315 g/10 oz canned creamed sweet corn
4 egg yolks
freshly ground black pepper
5 egg whites

1 Grease an 18 cm/7 in soufflé dish,
sprinkle with bread crumbs and set aside.

2 Melt butter in a saucepan and cook
onion and chilli over a medium heat for
10 minutes, or until onion is soft and
golden. Stir in flour and cook for 1 minute
longer. Remove pan from heat and
gradually stir in milk and corn. Return to
heat and cook, stirring constantly, until
mixture boils and thickens. Remove from
heat and beat in egg yolks one at a time.
Season to taste with black pepper.

3 Place egg whites in a bowl and beat
until stiff peaks form. Fold gently into
corn mixture.

4 Spoon soufflé mixture into prepared
dish and bake for 30-35 minutes or until
soufflé is puffed and golden. Serve
immediately.

Serves 4

Oven temperature
200°C, 400°F, Gas 6

To test if a soufflé is cooked,
shake the dish gently. If the
soufflé wobbles all over,
cook for 5 minutes longer.
Always serve a soufflé
immediately it is cooked.

CORN AND MUSHROOM ROULADE

Oven temperature
220°C, 425°F, Gas 7

60 g/2 oz butter
$^1/_3$ cup/60 g/2 oz wholemeal flour
$^3/_4$ cup/185 mL/6 fl oz milk
3 eggs, separated
125 g/4 oz canned creamed sweet corn

MUSHROOM FILLING
$^1/_3$ cup/90 mL/3 fl oz vegetable stock
or water
3 tablespoons sour cream
or natural yogurt
2 tablespoons chopped fresh basil
15 g/$^1/_2$ oz butter
185 g/6 oz mushrooms, finely chopped
1 onion, finely chopped
1 tablespoon flour

RED PEPPER SAUCE
30 g/1 oz butter
1 onion, chopped
2 teaspoons flour
1 cup/250 mL/8 fl oz vegetable stock
or water
200 g/6$^1/_2$ oz canned sweet red peppers,
drained and chopped or 2 red peppers,
roasted, skins removed and chopped

When folding egg whites into
a mixture, first mix in 2-3
tablespoons of the egg
whites to loosen the mixture.
Then add the remaining egg
whites and gently fold them
in, using a metal spoon or
spatula.

1 Melt butter in a saucepan and cook
flour for 1 minute. Gradually blend in
milk and cook over a medium heat,
stirring constantly, until mixture boils
and thickens. Whisk in egg yolks and
corn. Beat egg whites until stiff peaks
form and gently fold into corn mixture.
Spread mixture into a lightly greased and
lined 25 x 30 cm/10 x 12 in Swiss roll tin.
Bake for 15-20 minutes or until puffed
and golden.

2 To make filling, place stock or water,
sour cream or yogurt and basil in a bowl
and whisk to combine. Melt butter in a
saucepan and cook mushrooms and onion
for 5 minutes or until onion softens. Stir
in flour and cook for 1 minute. Gradually
stir in stock mixture and cook over a
medium heat, stirring constantly, until
mixture boils and thickens.

3 To make sauce, melt butter in a
saucepan and cook onion for 3 minutes.
Stir in flour and cook for 1 minute longer.
Gradually mix in stock or water and red
peppers, and cook over a medium heat,
stirring constantly, until sauce boils and
thickens.

4 Turn roulade onto a wire rack covered
with a clean teatowel and remove paper.
Quickly spread with warm filling and
gently roll up from the short side, with
the help of the teatowel. Serve roulade
sliced with warm sauce.

Serves 4

*Left: Corn and Mushroom Roulade,
Right: Leek and Apple Pie*

LEEK AND APPLE PIE

375 g/12 oz prepared shortcrust pastry

APPLE AND LEEK FILLING
15 g/^{1}/$_2$ oz butter
1 cooking apple, cored, peeled and sliced
3 small leeks, sliced
4 rashers bacon, chopped
^{1}/$_4$ teaspoon ground cloves
^{1}/$_4$ teaspoon ground nutmeg
60 g/2 oz blue vein cheese, crumbled
3 eggs, lightly beaten
^{3}/$_4$ cup/185 mL/6 fl oz cream (double)
2 tablespoons port (optional)
freshly ground black pepper

Serves 8

1   To make filling, melt butter in a frying pan and cook apple, leeks and bacon over a medium heat for 6-8 minutes or until apple softens. Add cloves and nutmeg and cook for 1 minute longer. Set aside to cool.

2   Roll out pastry on a lightly floured surface and line the base and sides of a lightly greased 23 cm/9 in flan tin. Prick base of pastry with a fork, line with nonstick baking paper and fill with uncooked rice. Bake for 10 minutes. Remove rice and paper.

3   Spread apple mixture over base of pastry case. Place cheese, eggs, cream, port (if used) and black pepper to taste in a bowl, mix to combine and carefully pour into pastry case. Reduce oven temperature to 180°C/350°F/Gas 4 and bake for 30-35 minutes or until pie is firm.

Oven temperature
220°C, 425°F, Gas 7

This pie is delicious hot, warm or cold.

VEGETABLE FLAN

Oven temperature
180°C, 350°F, Gas 4

185 g/6 oz prepared wholemeal
shortcrust pastry
30 g/1 oz butter
1 tablespoon flour
1 1/4 cups/315 mL/10 fl oz milk
315 g/10 oz canned sweet corn
kernels, drained
125 g/4 oz fresh or frozen peas, cooked
4 spring onions, chopped
freshly ground black pepper
2 eggs
125 g/4 oz grated tasty cheese
(mature Cheddar)

1 Roll out pastry to fit a 23 cm/9 in flan
tin. Prick pastry case with fork, line with
nonstick baking paper and fill with
uncooked rice. Bake for 8 minutes, then
remove rice and paper and bake for 10
minutes longer or until pastry is golden.

2 Melt butter in a saucepan and cook
flour for 1 minute. Gradually stir in milk
and cook over a medium heat, stirring
constantly, for 4-5 minutes or until
mixture boils and thickens. Add corn,
peas, spring onions and black pepper to
taste, then mix in eggs.

3 Pour corn mixture into pastry case,
sprinkle with cheese and bake for 30
minutes or until set and golden.

Serves 4

Did you know? The colour of
an eggshell depends on the
breed of the hen and has no
bearing on the nutritional
value of the egg.

Far left: Vegetable Flan
Left: Cheese and Chives Soufflé

CHEESE AND CHIVES SOUFFLES

60 g/2 oz butter
$^1/_2$ cup/60 g/2 oz flour
$1^1/_4$ cups/315 mL/10 fl oz hot milk
125 g/4 oz grated tasty cheese
(mature Cheddar)
1 teaspoon ground nutmeg
3 eggs, separated
2 tablespoons snipped fresh chives

1   Melt butter in a saucepan and cook flour over a medium heat, stirring constantly for 1 minute. Reduce heat, stir in hot milk and whisk over a low heat until sauce is smooth and thickens.

2   Remove pan from heat and set aside to cool for 10 minutes. Stir in cheese, nutmeg, egg yolks and chives.

3   Place egg whites in a bowl and beat until soft peaks form. Fold egg white mixture into sauce. Divide soufflé mixture between six greased and collared $^1/_2$ cup/ 185 mL/6 fl oz capacity soufflé dishes and bake for 15-20 minutes or until soufflés are puffed and golden.

Serves 6

Oven temperature
200°C, 400°F, Gas 6

For the best volume have egg whites at room temperature before beating. Egg whites for a soufflé should be beaten until they are stiff but not dry.

25

SPINACH ROULADE

Oven temperature
200°C, 400°F, Gas 6

250 g/8 oz frozen spinach, thawed
1 tablespoon flour
5 eggs, separated
15 g/¹/₂ oz butter
1 teaspoon ground nutmeg
freshly ground black pepper
2 tablespoons grated Parmesan cheese

MUSHROOM FILLING
30 g/1 oz butter
125 g/4 oz button mushrooms, sliced
3 spring onions, chopped
440 g/14 oz canned tomatoes, drained
and mashed
1 teaspoon chopped fresh oregano or
¹/₂ teaspoon dried oregano
2 teaspoons chopped fresh basil or
¹/₂ teaspoon dried basil
freshly ground black pepper

Eggs have always been a symbol of new life and prosperity. It is said that if you dream about eggs then the future will bring riches and good luck. However, beware if the eggs you dream about are broken or cracked, as this indicates you will quarrel with your lover.

Serves 6

1   Place spinach, flour, egg yolks, butter, nutmeg and black pepper to taste in a food processor or blender and process until combined. Transfer to a bowl.

2   Place egg whites in a bowl and beat until stiff peaks form, then mix 2 tablespoons of egg whites into spinach mixture. Fold remaining egg whites into spinach mixture. Spoon into a greased and lined 25 x 30 cm/10 x 12 in Swiss roll tin and cook for 12 minutes or until firm.

3   To make filling, melt butter in a frying pan and cook mushrooms over a medium heat for 1 minute. Add spring onions, tomatoes, oregano, basil and black pepper to taste, and cook for 3 minutes longer.

4   Turn roulade onto a teatowel, sprinkle with Parmesan cheese and roll up. Allow to stand for 1 minute. Unroll and spread with filling. Reroll and serve immediately.

Below: Vegetable Bake
Bottom Left: Spinach Roulade

VEGETABLE BAKE

2 zucchini (courgettes), grated
1 large potato, grated
1 green pepper, finely chopped
2 stalks celery, finely chopped
1 leek, thinly sliced
2 slices multigrain bread, crumbed
60 g/2 oz grated tasty cheese
(mature Cheddar)
3 eggs, lightly beaten
3 tablespoons finely chopped fresh dill
freshly ground black pepper

1   Place zucchini (courgettes), potato green pepper, celery, leek, bread crumbs, cheese, eggs and dill in a large bowl and mix to combine. Season to taste with black pepper.

2   Spoon mixture into a lightly greased ovenproof dish and bake for 45-50 minutes or until firm.

Serves 4

Oven temperature
200°C, 400°F, Gas 6

This Vegetable Bake is delicious eaten hot, warm or cold. Cold, it makes a wonderful picnic dish and is delicious accompanied by a tomato salad.

SPINACH PANCAKE STACK

Oven temperature
180°C, 350°F, Gas 4

500 g/1 lb jar Italian tomato sauce
4 slices ham

SPINACH PANCAKES
250 g/8 oz frozen spinach, thawed
$^3/4$ cup/90 g/3 oz flour
1 egg
$1^1/4$ cups/315 mL/10 fl oz milk
30 g/1 oz butter, melted

CHEESE SAUCE
45 g/1$^1/2$ oz butter
2 tablespoons flour
1 cup/250 mL/8 fl oz chicken stock
$^2/3$ cup/170 mL/5$^1/2$ fl oz cream (double)
4 tablespoons grated Parmesan cheese

1 Place tomato sauce in a saucepan and bring to the boil over a medium heat, then reduce to simmering and cook until reduced by half.

2 To make pancakes, place spinach, flour, egg, milk and butter in a food processor or blender and process to combine. Pour one-fifth of the batter into a hot, lightly greased 23 cm/9 in frying pan and cook over a medium heat for 2-3 minutes or until bubbles form on the surface. Turn pancake and cook other side until golden. Remove pancake from pan and set aside. Repeat with remaining pancake mixture to make five pancakes in all.

3 To assemble pancake stack, place one pancake in a lightly greased 23 cm/9 in ovenproof dish, top with ham, spread with tomato sauce and top with a second pancake. Repeat layers to use all ingredients, ending with a pancake. Cover and bake for 10-15 minutes or until heated through.

4 To make sauce, melt butter in a saucepan and cook flour over a medium heat, stirring, for 1 minute. Stir in stock and cream and cook, stirring constantly, for 4-5 minutes or until sauce boils and thickens. Remove sauce from heat and stir in Parmesan cheese. Serve with pancake stack cut into wedges.

Serves 4

Pancake stacks always look impressive and make a satisfying main meal. The stack can be prepared ahead of time and reheated while making the Cheese Sauce – great for those late-night dinners or after-the-show suppers.

'Did you know? The largest pancake ever cooked used 5274 eggs, 2322 kilograms of flour, 442 litres of milk and was 7.5 metres in diameter.'

Summer Vegetable Quiche

SUMMER VEGETABLE QUICHE

2 eggplant (aubergines), cut into
$^1/_2$ cm/$^1/_4$ in cubes
$^1/_4$ cup/60 mL/2 fl oz olive oil
1 large onion, chopped
4 zucchini (courgettes), cut into
$^1/_2$ cm/$^1/_4$ in slices
2 tomatoes, peeled and chopped
6 eggs
$^1/_4$ cup/60 mL/2 fl oz milk
60 g/2 oz grated Parmesan cheese
$^1/_4$ cup/15 g/$^1/_2$ oz bread crumbs, made
from stale bread
2 tablespoons snipped fresh chives
3 tablespoons grated tasty cheese
(mature Cheddar)

Serves 6

1 Place eggplant (aubergines) in a colander set over a bowl, sprinkle with salt and set aside to drain for 20 minutes. Wash and pat dry using absorbent kitchen paper.

2 Heat 1 tablespoon oil in a large frying pan and cook onion for 3-4 minutes. Add remaining oil, eggplant (aubergines) and zucchini (courgettes) and cook, stirring frequently, for 5 minutes longer. Stir in tomatoes and simmer, stirring occasionally, for 20 minutes or until mixture is reduced and thickened.

3 Place eggs and milk in a large mixing bowl and whisk to combine. Stir in Parmesan cheese, bread crumbs and chives. Stir egg mixture into vegetable mixture and spoon into a lightly greased 23 cm/9 in ovenproof dish. Sprinkle with tasty cheese (mature Cheddar) and bake for 30 minutes or until set.

Oven temperature
180°C, 350°F, Gas 4

This crustless quiche combines all the best flavours of summer to give a dish that is perfect for family meals or casual entertaining. Accompany with garlic or herb bread and a crisp green salad to make a complete meal.

LIGHT MEALS

As the basis for a light meal eggs are hard to beat. Nutritious and delicious would be the best way to describe the recipes in this chapter. No matter whether it's the Tossed Egg Salad, Mini Salmon Quiches or the ever-popular Indian Egg Curry, most of these dishes need only crusty bread and a salad to make a complete meal.

Coconut Curried Eggs

COCONUT CURRIED EGGS

8 hard-boiled eggs, halved

COCONUT CURRY SAUCE
30 g/1 oz butter
1 onion, chopped
2 teaspoons curry powder
1 teaspoon ground cumin
1 tablespoon cornflour
1 cup/250 mL/8 fl oz chicken stock
1 cup/250 mL/8 fl oz coconut milk
2 tablespoons lemon juice

1   To make sauce, melt butter in a saucepan and cook onion for 3-4 minutes or until soft. Stir in curry powder, cumin and cornflour, and cook for 1 minute longer.

2   Place stock, coconut milk and lemon juice in a bowl and mix to combine. Stir stock mixture into pan and cook over a medium heat, stirring constantly, for 4-5 minutes or until sauce boils and thickens.

3   Place eggs in a large ovenproof dish, pour curry sauce over and bake for 10-15 minutes or until heated.

Serves 4

Oven temperature
180°C, 350°F, Gas 4

Serve these curried eggs with boiled white or brown rice tossed with parsley.

SAVOURY BAKED CUSTARDS

125 g/4 oz fresh or frozen peas
15 g/^{1}/2 oz butter
1 onion, finely chopped
2 cloves garlic, crushed
2 tablespoons chopped fresh basil
2 eggs, lightly beaten
^{1}/2 cup/125 mL/4 fl oz cream (double)
^{3}/4 cup/185 mL/6 fl oz milk
^{1}/4 teaspoon ground nutmeg
60 g/2 oz ham, finely chopped

1   Boil, steam or microwave peas until just tender. Drain, refresh under cold running water, drain again and set aside.

2   Melt butter in a large saucepan and cook onion and garlic over a medium heat, stirring, for 2-3 minutes or until onion is just soft. Add peas and basil and cook for 1 minute longer. Transfer mixture to a food processor or blender and process until smooth. With machine running, add eggs, cream, milk and nutmeg and process to combine. Stir in ham.

3   Divide mixture between four ^{1}/2 cup/ 125 mL/4 fl oz capacity ramekins and place in an ovenproof dish with enough hot water to come halfway up the sides of the ramekins. Bake for 45 minutes or until custards are firm.

Serves 4

Oven temperature
160°C, 325°F, Gas 3

It is important that a baked custard such as this one is not cooked at too high a temperature or for too long. Placing the ramekins in a dish of water or 'bain-marie' helps to protect the custard from fierce heat. If cooked for too long or at too high a temperature, the egg protein coagulates and shrinks, and holes form in the custard. The liquid then seeps out and the texture of the custard is ruined.

Open Bearnaise Burgers

2 English muffins, split and toasted
4 lettuce leaves

BEEF PATTIES
500 g/1 lb lean beef mince
1 teaspoon finely grated lemon rind
1 small onion, finely chopped
1 clove garlic, crushed
3 teaspoons finely chopped fresh
tarragon or 1 teaspoon dried tarragon
1 egg
$^1/_4$ cup/30 g/1 oz dried bread crumbs

BEARNAISE SAUCE
3 egg yolks
3 teaspoons finely chopped fresh
tarragon or 1 teaspoon dried tarragon
1 tablespoon tarragon vinegar
1 tablespoon lemon juice
250 g/8 oz butter

1   To make patties, place beef mince, lemon rind, onion, garlic, tarragon, egg and bread crumbs in a bowl and mix to combine. Divide mixture into twelve and shape into small patties. Cook patties under a preheated grill for 4-5 minutes each side or until cooked to your liking. Remove patties from grill, drain on absorbent kitchen paper and keep warm.

2   To make sauce, place egg yolks, tarragon, vinegar and lemon juice in a food processor or blender and process until smooth. Melt butter until it is hot and bubbling. With machine running, slowly pour in melted butter and process until sauce is thick.

3   To assemble, top each muffin half with a lettuce leaf, three patties and a little sauce. Serve immediately.

Serves 4

These sophisticated mini burgers are sure to be popular with everyone who likes good food.

Eggs in a Mushroom Nest

Oven temperature
180°C, 350°F, Gas 4

30 g/1 oz butter
4 large flat or open cap mushrooms,
stalks removed
1 onion, finely chopped
$^1/_2$ red pepper, finely chopped
1 clove garlic, crushed
4 small eggs
4 tablespoons cream (double)
4 tablespoons grated Gruyère cheese

1   Melt butter in a frying pan and cook mushrooms over a medium heat, skin side down, for 1 minute. Remove mushrooms from pan and place in a lightly greased ovenproof dish.

2   Add onion, red pepper and garlic to pan and cook, stirring, for 5 minutes or until onions are soft. Divide onion mixture between mushrooms and, using the back of a spoon, make a depression in the mixture to form a nest. Break an egg into each mushroom. Top each egg with 1 tablespoon cream and sprinkle with 1 tablespoon cheese. Bake for 10-15 minutes or until egg whites are set and cheese is melted.

Large flat mushrooms make the perfect cooking and serving container for baked eggs. For a complete meal serve with a tossed green salad and wholemeal rolls.

Serves 4

INDIVIDUAL FRITTATAS

15 g/^{1}/$_2$ oz butter
1 onion, chopped
1 clove garlic, crushed
2 slices ham, chopped
^{1}/$_4$ teaspoon finely chopped
fresh red chilli
1 red pepper, finely chopped
2 spring onions, chopped
125 g/4 oz pineapple pieces, drained
1 tablespoon finely chopped
fresh parsley
4 eggs
^{3}/$_4$ cup/185 mL/6 fl oz milk
30 g/1 oz grated tasty cheese
(mature Cheddar)

1 Melt butter in a large frying pan and cook onion, garlic, ham, chilli, red pepper and spring onions over a medium heat for 3-4 minutes or until onion is soft. Stir in pineapple pieces and parsley, remove pan from heat and set aside to cool for 10 minutes.

2 Place eggs, milk and cheese in a bowl and mix to combine. Stir in ham mixture. Divide mixture between four 10 cm/4 in lightly greased flan tins and bake for 20-25 minutes or until set.

Serves 4

Oven temperature
180°C, 350°F, Gas 4

*Open Béarnaise Burgers,
Eggs in a Mushroom Nest*

POTATO AND EGG SALAD

If hard-boiled eggs are overcooked, a dark ring will form around the yolk. This is because the iron in the egg yolk combines with the sulphur in the egg white and the result is a greyish-black iron sulphide ring. To prevent this, avoid overcooking eggs and cool the unshelled cooked eggs quickly in cold water.

1 kg/2 lb baby potatoes, scrubbed
2 tablespoons chopped fresh parsley
6 hard-boiled eggs, quartered
1 onion, thinly sliced

AVOCADO DRESSING
1 avocado, stoned, peeled and chopped
1 clove garlic, crushed
1 tablespoon lemon juice
125 g/4 oz sour cream or natural yogurt
2 drops Tabasco sauce
1 teaspoon honey

1   Boil, steam or microwave potatoes until just tender. Drain and refresh under cold running water. Place potatoes, parsley, eggs and onion in a large salad bowl.

2   To make dressing, place avocado, garlic, lemon juice, sour cream or yogurt, Tabasco sauce and honey in a food processor or blender and process until smooth. Just prior to serving, spoon dressing over salad.

Serves 6

Potato and Egg Salad

MINI SALMON QUICHES

350 g/11 oz prepared wholemeal
shortcrust pastry
15 g/^{1}/$_2$ oz butter
1 onion, finely chopped
220 g/7 oz canned salmon, drained
and flaked
2 eggs, lightly beaten
^{3}/$_4$ cup/185 mL/6 fl oz milk
^{1}/$_4$ teaspoon ground nutmeg
2 teaspoons chopped fresh dill
freshly ground black pepper
60 g/2 oz grated tasty cheese
(mature Cheddar)
1 tablespoon snipped fresh chives

1 Roll out pastry on a lightly floured
surface and use to line six lightly greased
10 cm/4 in flan tins.

2 Melt butter in a frying pan and cook
onion for 4-5 minutes or until soft. Divide
onion mixture between flans and spread
over pastry. Top with salmon.

3 Place eggs, milk, nutmeg, dill and
black pepper to taste in a bowl and mix to
combine. Divide egg mixture between
flans, sprinkle with cheese and chives and
bake for 20 minutes or until filling is firm.

Makes 6

Oven temperature
200°C, 400°F, Gas 6

You might like to make
Spinach and Ham Quiches.
To make these, boil, steam or
microwave 125 g/4 oz
chopped spinach until
tender. Divide into four
portions and spread over
base of flans. Divide 125 g/
4 oz chopped ham and 3
tablespoons finely chopped
red pepper between flans,
then continue as in recipe.

Tossed Egg Salad

TOSSED EGG SALAD

1 lettuce, leaves separated and washed
10 stuffed green olives, halved
5 black olives, pitted and sliced
4 hard-boiled eggs, sliced
1 red pepper, cut into thin strips
2 stalks celery, cut into thin strips

HONEY DRESSING
2 tablespoons red wine vinegar
1 teaspoon honey
1 tablespoon lime juice
1 teaspoon olive oil

Ideal for weight watchers, this salad is an elegant lunch or supper dish. For a complete meal, accompany with crusty bread and finish with a piece of fresh fruit.

1   Arrange lettuce, green and black olives, eggs, red pepper and celery on a large platter.

2   To make dressing, place vinegar, honey, lime juice and oil in a screwtop jar and shake well to combine. Drizzle over salad and serve immediately.

Serves 4 as a light meal

CORN AND HAM QUICHE

125 g/4 oz prepared shortcrust pastry
125 g/4 oz canned sweet corn kernels,
drained
125 g/4 oz ham, chopped
3 spring onions, finely chopped
90 g/3 oz grated tasty cheese
(mature Cheddar)
³/4 cup/185 g/6 oz sour cream
¹/2 cup/125 mL/4 fl oz milk
3 eggs

1 Roll out pastry and use to line a lightly greased 23 cm/9 in flan tin. Prick pastry with a fork, line with nonstick baking paper and fill with uncooked rice. Bake for 5 minutes, then remove rice and paper and bake for 10 minutes longer or until pastry is golden.

2 Place sweet corn, ham, spring onions and cheese in a bowl and mix to combine. Spread sweet corn mixture over base of pastry case. Place sour cream, milk and eggs in a bowl and beat to combine. Pour over sweet corn mixture, reduce oven temperature to 180°C/350°F/Gas 4 and bake for 30 minutes or until top is golden and filling firm.

Oven temperature
200°C, 400°F, Gas 6

A quiche is an all-time favourite light meal. Whether you choose to serve this one hot, warm or cold, you can be sure that it will be popular. Leftovers can go in lunch boxes the next day.

Corn and Ham Quiche

Serves 6

Vegetable and Egg Stir-fry

125 g/4 oz snow peas (mangetout), trimmed
185 g/6 oz asparagus spears, cut into 5 cm/2 in pieces
3 eggs
1 teaspoon sesame oil
$^1/_4$ cup/60 mL/2 fl oz water
1 teaspoon dry sherry
1 teaspoon soy sauce
freshly ground black pepper
1 tablespoon vegetable oil
3 spring onions, chopped

1 Boil, steam or microwave snow peas (mangetout) and asparagus separately until just tender. Drain and refresh under cold running water. Drain again and set aside.

2 Place eggs, sesame oil, water, sherry, soy sauce and black pepper to taste in a bowl and whisk lightly to combine.

3 Heat vegetable oil in a wok or frying pan, add egg mixture and stir-fry for 1 minute or until egg mixture just begins to set. Add snow peas (mangetout), asparagus and spring onions and stir-fry for 1 minute longer. Serve immediately.

Serves 2

Often called Egg Foo Yung and traditionally made with prawns, fish or beef, this popular recipe is delicious just made with vegetables.

Blue Cheese Omelette

15 g/$^1/_2$ oz butter
2 eggs
2 teaspoons water
freshly ground black pepper

CHEESE AND APPLE FILLING
15 g/$^1/_2$ oz butter
$^1/_2$ small green apple, cored and thinly sliced
30 g/1 oz blue cheese, crumbled
1 teaspoon snipped fresh chives

1 To make filling, melt butter in a small frying pan and cook apple over a low heat for 2-3 minutes or until just heated through. Remove pan from heat, set aside and keep warm.

2 To make omelette, melt butter in a small frying pan. Place eggs, water and black pepper to taste in a small bowl and whisk to combine. Pour egg mixture into frying pan and cook over a medium heat, continually drawing in the edge of the omelette with a fork during cooking, until no liquid remains and the omelette is lightly set.

3 Top half the omelette with apple slices, cheese and chives and fold in half. Slip onto a plate and serve immediately.

Serves 1

Cheese and apples are natural partners; as a filling in this omelette, they are an extra-special combination.

INDIAN EGG CURRY

6 hard-boiled eggs, halved lengthwise

CURRY SAUCE
1 tablespoon vegetable oil
1 large onion, finely chopped
1 clove garlic, crushed
1 tablespoon finely chopped
fresh root ginger
1 teaspoon ground cumin
1 teaspoon ground coriander
1/2 teaspoon chilli powder
1 teaspoon ground turmeric
400 g/14 oz canned tomatoes,
undrained and mashed
1/2 cup/125 mL/4 fl oz coconut milk
freshly ground black pepper

Indian Egg Curry,
Vegetable and Egg Stir-fry

1 To make sauce, heat oil in a frying pan and cook onion, garlic and ginger over a medium heat for 5 minutes or until onion softens. Stir in cumin, coriander, chilli powder and turmeric, and cook for 2 minutes longer.

2 Add tomatoes and coconut milk, bring to the boil, then reduce heat and simmer for 15 minutes or until sauce reduces and thickens. Season to taste with black pepper.

3 Place eggs in a shallow baking dish and spoon sauce over. Cover and bake for 20 minutes or until heated through.

Serves 6

Oven temperature
180°C, 350°F, Gas 4

A delicious egg curry that combines all the tastes of India. For a complete meal, accompany with steamed or boiled white or brown rice.

PICKLED VEGETABLE OMELETTE

2 tablespoons peanut or groundnut oil
250 g/8 oz lean beef mince
2 tablespoons bottled Chinese mixed
vegetables (tung chai), drained
and chopped
1 teaspoon honey
2 tablespoons soy sauce
6 spring onions, finely chopped
6 eggs, lightly beaten

1 Heat 1 tablespoon oil in a frying pan and stir-fry beef mince, vegetables, honey, soy sauce and spring onions for 3-4 minutes or until cooked. Remove from pan, set aside and keep warm.

2 Heat remaining oil in a clean frying pan, pour in one-quarter of the beaten eggs. Swirl pan over heat to make a thin omelette. Spoon one-quarter of the meat mixture into the centre of the omelette and fold over the edges.

3 Remove omelette from pan, set aside and keep warm. Repeat with remaining eggs and meat mixture. Cut omelettes into slices and serve immediately.

Serves 4

The Chinese mixed vegetables used as the filling for this omelette are available from most Oriental supermarkets.

*Left: Eggplant (Aubergine) Soufflé
Far Left: Pickled Vegetable
Omelette*

EGGPLANT (AUBERGINE) SOUFFLE

75 g/2$^1/_2$ oz butter
2 cloves garlic, crushed
1 onion, finely chopped
1 large eggplant (aubergine), peeled and
finely chopped
$^1/_2$ cup/125 mL/4 fl oz water
2 cups/500 mL/16 fl oz milk
7 eggs
2 tablespoons flour
125 g/4 oz grated tasty cheese
(mature Cheddar)

Serves 4

1   Melt 45 g/1$^1/_2$ oz butter in a large
frying pan and cook garlic and onion for
2 minutes. Add eggplant (aubergine) and
cook for 5 minutes longer. Add water to
pan, cover and simmer over a low heat for
1 hour, stirring frequently, and adding
more water if necessary.

2   Place 1$^1/_2$ cups/375 mL/12 fl oz milk
and remaining butter in a saucepan and
bring to the boil. Place remaining milk,
5 egg yolks, 2 whole eggs and flour in a
bowl and whisk to combine. Slowly whisk
egg mixture into boiling milk, reduce heat
and cook, whisking constantly, until sauce
thickens. Remove pan from heat and stir
in eggplant (aubergine) mixture and
cheese.

3   Place 5 egg whites in a bowl and beat
until stiff peaks form. Fold egg whites into
sauce, then spoon into a lightly greased
20 cm/8 in soufflé dish with collar attached.
Bake for 35 minutes . Serve immediately.

Oven temperature
180°C, 350°F, Gas 4

The name 'eggplant'
originated from the white
variety of the fruit being
about the same size, colour
and shape as an egg.
Like tomatoes and sweet
peppers, eggplant
(aubergine) is a fruit that is
treated as a vegetable.

41

DESSERTS

Many desserts rely on eggs to give them their texture and flavour. This chapter presents the best of egg desserts, so whether you want a traditional Lemon Chiffon Pie, an airy pavlova or, everyone's favourite, a sweet soufflé, you will find it here.

Lemon Delicious Pudding

Lemon Delicious Pudding

1 cup/220 g/7 oz caster sugar
125 g/4 oz butter, softened
^{1}/2 cup/60 g/2 oz self-raising flour, sifted
1 tablespoon finely grated lemon rind
1 tablespoon finely grated orange rind
2 tablespoons lemon juice
2 tablespoons orange juice
2 eggs, separated
1 cup/250 mL/8 fl oz milk

1 Place sugar and butter in a bowl and beat until light and fluffy. Mix in flour, lemon and orange rinds, lemon and orange juices.

2 Place egg yolks and milk in a small bowl and whisk to combine. Mix into citrus mixture.

3 Beat egg whites until stiff peaks form then fold into batter. Spoon into a greased 4 cup/1 litre/1^3/4 pt capacity ovenproof dish. Place dish in a baking pan with enough boiling water to come halfway up the sides of the dish. Bake for 45 minutes or until cooked. Serve hot with cream or ice cream if desired.

Serves 6

Oven temperature
180°C, 350°F, Gas 4

One of those magic puddings – as the pudding cooks it separates to give a layer of fluffy sponge over a tangy citrus sauce.

Whisky Bread and Butter Pudding

6 peaches, peeled, stoned and sliced
45 g/1^1/2 oz butter, softened
12 slices white bread, crusts removed
3 teaspoons ground cinnamon

TOFFEE
^{3}/4 cup/185 g/6 oz sugar
^{3}/4 cup/185 mL/6 fl oz water

WHISKY CUSTARD
3 eggs
^{2}/3 cup/140 g/4^1/2 oz caster sugar
1 cup/250 mL/8 fl oz milk, scalded
1 cup/250 mL/8 fl oz cream, scalded
2 tablespoons whisky

1 To make toffee, place sugar and water in a small saucepan and cook over a low heat, stirring, until sugar dissolves. Increase heat and simmer until toffee is a golden colour. Pour toffee into base of a well-greased 25 cm/10 in round ovenproof dish and set aside.

2 Poach or microwave peaches until just tender. Drain well and set aside.

3 To make custard, place eggs and sugar in a bowl and whisk to combine. Whisk in milk, cream and whisky.

4 Butter bread on one side, then cut into triangles. Place a layer of bread in base of ovenproof dish then top with a layer of peaches and sprinkle with cinnamon. Repeat layers, until bread, peaches and cinnamon are all used, ending with a bread layer. Carefully pour custard over the layers. Place dish in a large baking dish with enough hot water to come halfway up the sides of the dish and bake for 50-60 minutes or until custard is set. Stand for 15 minutes before turning out and serving.

Serves 8

Oven temperature
180°C, 350°F, Gas 4

Poured into the base of the baking dish, toffee adds a delicious flavour to this traditional English pudding. Baking it in a pan of hot water ensures a smooth, creamy custard.
If fresh peaches are unavailable drained canned peaches can be used instead – in which case there is no need to cook them.

FLOATING ISLANDS

6 eggs, separated
1 cup/220 g/7 oz caster sugar
3 cups/750 mL/1 ¹/4 pt milk
4 teaspoons vanilla essence
mint leaves

TOFFEE
1 cup/250 g/8 oz sugar
¹/3 cup/90 mL/3 fl oz water

Also called Snow Eggs this romantic dessert is an example of poached meringues. The custard and meringues can be made ahead of time and chilled, but the toffee should be made and spun within an hour of serving.

1   Place egg whites in a bowl and beat until soft peaks form. Gradually beat in ¹/2 cup/100 g/3¹/2 oz caster sugar and beat until sugar dissolves and stiff peaks form. This will take 7-10 minutes.

2   Place milk and vanilla essence in a saucepan and bring to the boil, then reduce heat to simmering. Using 2 dessertspoons, shape spoonfuls of egg white mixture and poach in milk for 2 minutes. Using a slotted spoon, remove meringue and place on absorbent kitchen paper. Reserve poaching liquid.

3   Place egg yolks and remaining sugar in a large bowl and beat until thick and creamy. Gradually pour reserved poaching liquid into egg yolk mixture and beat for 3 minutes longer. Transfer custard mixture to a large saucepan and cook over a low heat, stirring constantly and taking care not to allow the mixture to boil, for 8-10 minutes or until custard thickens.

4   To make toffee, place sugar and water in a small saucepan and cook over a medium heat, stirring constantly until sugar dissolves. Continue to cook, without stirring, until mixture is golden. Remove pan from heat and set aside to stand until bubbles subside. Place meringues on a pool of custard. Spin toffee and use to decorate dessert.

Serves 4

Floating Islands

Lemon Chiffon Pie

LEMON CHIFFON PIE

250 g/8 oz oatmeal biscuits, crushed
75 g/2^1/$_2$ oz butter, melted

LEMON FILLING
4 eggs, separated
^{3}/$_4$ cup/170 g/5^1/$_2$ oz caster sugar
1 tablespoon finely grated lemon rind
^{1}/$_2$ cup/125 mL/4 fl oz lemon juice
2 teaspoons gelatine
^{1}/$_4$ cup/60 mL/2 fl oz white wine

1   Place crushed biscuits and butter in a bowl and mix to combine. Press mixture into a lightly greased 23 cm/9 in springform tin, pressing crumbs as far as possible up the sides of the tin. Chill biscuit crumb case until ready to fill.

2   To make filling, place egg yolks, ^{1}/$_2$ cup/100 g/3^1/$_2$ oz sugar and lemon rind in a bowl and beat until light and fluffy. Place ^{1}/$_4$ cup/60 mL/2 fl oz lemon juice in a small saucepan and bring to the boil. Continue beating egg yolk mixture while pouring in hot lemon juice in a thin steady stream.

3   Place gelatine and wine in a small bowl and dissolve over a saucepan of simmering water. Stir gelatine mixture into egg yolk mixture.

4   Place egg whites in a bowl and beat until stiff peaks form. Add remaining sugar and beat for 3 minutes longer. Fold egg white mixture into egg yolk mixture, then spoon filling into biscuit crumb case. Refrigerate for 2-3 hours or until set.

Serves 8

You might like to try a Lime Chiffon Pie for a change. Just replace half the lemon juice with lime juice and replace the lemon rind with lime rind.

SABAYON WITH BERRIES

3 egg yolks
¹/4 cup/60 g/2 oz caster sugar
2 tablespoons Cointreau
(orange liqueur)
1 teaspoon gelatine
¹/4 cup/60 mL/2 fl oz white wine
¹/2 cup/125 mL/4 fl oz cream (double),
lightly whipped
250 g/8 oz fresh berries of your choice

1   Place egg yolks, sugar and Cointreau
(orange liqueur) in a bowl and place
over a saucepan of boiling water. Cook,
whisking mixture constantly, for 3
minutes or until thick. Remove pan from
heat and set aside.

2   Place gelatine and wine in a small
bowl and dissolve over a saucepan of
simmering water. Whisk gelatine mixture
into egg mixture and continue to whisk
until mixture is cool.

3   Fold cream into egg yolk mixture,
spoon into individual serving glasses and
chill. Serve with berries.

Serves 4

Sweet sabayon is the French
version of the Italian dessert
zabaglione. In this recipe the
basic sabayon sauce is set
with gelatine to make a
delectable summer dessert.

Sabayon with Berries

Passion Fruit Pavlova

PASSION FRUIT PAVLOVA

6 egg whites
1 cup/220 g/7 oz caster sugar
¹/₄ teaspoon cream of tartar
2 teaspoons cornflour
1¹/₂ cups/375 mL/12 fl oz cream
(double), whipped
pulp 4 passion fruit
fresh mint leaves, cut into fine strips

Serves 8

1 Place egg whites in a large mixing bowl and beat until soft peaks form. Gradually add sugar, beating well after each addition until mixture is thick and glossy.

2 Fold cream of tartar and cornflour into egg white mixture.

3 Grease and line the base and sides of a 23 cm/9 in springform tin with nonstick baking paper, then lightly dust with extra cornflour. Spoon meringue into tin and spread out evenly. Bake for 1¹/₂ hours, then turn off oven and allow pavlova to cool for 30 minutes with oven door ajar. Remove pavlova from oven and set aside to cool completely.

4 Top cold pavlova with cream and decorate with passion fruit pulp and mint strips.

Oven temperature
120°C, 250°F, Gas ¹/₂

Both Australia and New Zealand claim to have created this truly marvellous dessert. However, both agree that it is named after the famous Russian ballerina, Anna Pavlova.

*Right: Creamy Vanilla Custards
Far Right: Crème Caramels*

CREAMY VANILLA CUSTARDS

4 egg yolks
$^{1}/_{3}$ cup/75 g/2$^{1}/_{2}$ oz caster sugar
**1$^{1}/_{2}$ cups/375 mL/12 fl oz cream
(double)**
3 teaspoons vanilla essence

CHOCOLATE STRAWBERRIES
250 g/8 oz strawberries
100 g/3$^{1}/_{2}$ oz dark chocolate, melted

1   To prepare strawberries, holding the stalk, dip each strawberry in chocolate to partially coat. Place on nonstick baking paper and allow chocolate to set at room temperature.

2   Place egg yolks and sugar in a bowl and beat for 2 minutes. Place cream in a saucepan and bring just to simmering, then remove from heat and slowly pour into egg mixture, while continuing to whisk vigorously. Stir in vanilla essence, then transfer custard to a clean saucepan and cook over a low heat without boiling, stirring constantly for 5-10 minutes or until custard thickens. Remove pan from heat and set aside to cool slightly.

3   Spoon custard into individual serving glasses and allow to cool completely. Serve accompanied with Chocolate Strawberries.

Serves 4

Gentle cooking for custard is essential or the custard will curdle. To ensure success you may wish to place the bowl over a saucepan of simmering water, or make the custard in a double boiler, rather than cooking it over a direct heat.

CREME CARAMELS

4 eggs, lightly beaten
1 teaspoon vanilla essence
$^1/_4$ cup/60 g/2 oz caster sugar
$^1/_2$ cup/60 g/2 oz milk powder, sifted
2 cups/500 mL/16 fl oz milk, scalded

CARAMEL
$^1/_2$ cup/125 mL/4 fl oz water
$^1/_2$ cup/125 g/4 oz sugar

1   To make Caramel, place water and sugar in a small, heavy-based saucepan and cook over a low heat, stirring constantly until sugar dissolves. Bring to the boil and boil, without stirring, until mixture turns a light golden brown. Pour

into six lightly greased $^1/_2$ cup/125 mL/ 4 fl oz capacity ramekins.

2   Place eggs, vanilla essence, sugar and milk powder in a mixing bowl and beat until sugar dissolves. Whisk in milk, then pour into ramekins.

3   Place ramekins in a baking dish with enough boiling water to come halfway up sides of ramekins and bake for 20 minutes, or until a knife inserted into the centre of custard comes out clean.

4   Remove ramekins from baking dish and set aside to cool. Chill before serving. To serve, invert chilled custards onto serving plates.

Serves 6

Oven temperature
180°C, 350°F, Gas 4

To scald milk or cream, rinse a small heavy-based saucepan with cold water, add the milk or cream and bring almost to the boil over a low heat, stirring occasionally. Scalding will help prevent curdling during cooking.

PASSION FRUIT SOUFFLE

Oven temperature
180°C, 350°F, Gas 4

Individual soufflés are the perfect dessert after a rich or spicy main meal. While the actual mixing and cooking of the soufflés has to be left until just before serving, the Nectarine Cream and preparation of the dishes can be done in advance.

softened butter
caster sugar
125 g/4 oz passion fruit pulp
$^2/_3$ cup/100 g/3$^1/_2$ oz icing sugar
2 egg yolks
1 tablespoon orange juice
6 egg whites

NECTARINE CREAM
2 very ripe nectarines, peeled
and stones removed
1$^1/_4$ cups/315 mL/10 fl oz cream
(double)
2 tablespoons icing sugar
2 tablespoons Grand Marnier
(orange liqueur)

1   Brush four 1$^1/_2$ cup/375 mL/12 fl oz capacity soufflé dishes with butter then sprinkle with caster sugar. Turn dishes upside down to allow excess sugar to fall out.

2   Place passion fruit pulp, $^1/_2$ cup/75 g/ 2$^1/_2$ oz icing sugar, egg yolks and orange juice in a large bowl and mix well to combine. Place egg whites in a mixing bowl and beat until soft peaks form, add remaining icing sugar and beat until just combined. Mix one-quarter egg white mixture into the passion fruit mixture, then gently fold in the remaining egg whites. Spoon into prepared soufflé dishes and bake for 8-10 minutes or until well risen and golden.

3   To make Nectarine Cream, place nectarine flesh in a food processor or blender and process to purée. Place cream, icing sugar and Grand Marnier (orange liqueur) in a bowl and beat until soft peaks form. Gently fold cream mixture into nectarine purée. Chill until ready to serve.

4   To serve, dust soufflés with icing sugar and accompany with Nectarine Cream.

Serves 4

Left: Passion Fruit Soufflé
Right: Blinis and Strawberries

BLINIS AND STRAWBERRIES

1 cup/250 mL/8 fl oz milk, warmed
1 teaspoon caster sugar
15 g/$^1/_2$ oz active dry yeast
3 eggs, separated
$^1/_2$ cup/125 g/4 oz sour cream
1$^1/_4$ cups/155 g/5 oz flour, sifted
30 g/1 oz butter
250 g/8 oz strawberries, quartered

STRAWBERRY SAUCE
250 g/8 oz strawberries
3 tablespoons Cointreau
(orange liqueur)

1 Place milk, sugar and yeast in a bowl and set aside to stand for 10 minutes or until yeast is frothy. Place egg yolks and sour cream in a bowl and whisk to combine. Stir in yeast mixture.

2 Whisk flour into yeast mixture, cover with a damp teatowel and set aside to stand in a warm place for 1 hour.

3 Place egg whites in a bowl and beat until soft peaks form. Fold egg whites into yeast mixture. Heat butter in a large frying pan and cook tablespoons of mixture for 1 minute each side or until golden. Set aside and keep warm.

4 To make sauce, place strawberries and Cointreau (orange liqueur) in a food processor or blender and process until smooth. Push strawberry mixture through a sieve. Serve blinis with fresh strawberries and Strawberry Sauce.

Serves 4

Originally savoury pancakes, blinis are also delicious served with fruit and a fruit sauce, as in this recipe. You might also like to make them using different types of flour such as corn meal (polenta), wholemeal or buckwheat flour. Each tastes a little different but all are wonderful whether served as a sweet or savoury dish.

MINIATURE PARIS BREST

Oven temperature
220°C, 425°F, Gas 7

CHOUX PASTRY
1 cup/250 mL/8 fl oz water
75 g/2$^{1}/_{2}$ oz butter, cut into small pieces
$^{3}/_{4}$ cup/90 g/3 oz flour, sifted
3 eggs

FILLING
$^{3}/_{4}$ cup/185 mL/6 fl oz cream (double), whipped
250 g/8 oz diced fresh fruit

TOFFEE
1 cup/250 g/8 oz sugar
$^{1}/_{3}$ cup/90 mL/3 fl oz water

1   To make pastry, place water and butter in a saucepan and slowly bring to the boil. As soon as the mixture boils, quickly stir in flour, using a wooden spoon. Cook over a low heat, stirring constantly, for 2 minutes or until mixture is smooth and leaves sides of pan. Remove from heat and set aside to cool slightly. Beat in eggs one at a time, beating well after each addition until mixture is light and glossy.

2   Line baking trays with nonstick baking paper and trace 5 cm/2 in circles on it. Spoon pastry mixture into a piping bag fitted with a 1 cm/$^{1}/_{2}$ in plain nozzle. Turn paper over and pipe two rows of pastry, one on top of the other, inside the traced circles. Bake for 8 minutes. Prop oven door open using the handle of a wooden spoon and cook pastries for 10 minutes longer, or until golden and crisp. Remove from tray and cool on a wire rack. Split pastries in half using a bread knife. Return to the oven and bake at 120°C/250°F/Gas $^{1}/_{2}$ for 5 minutes or until pastries dry out. Set aside to cool completely.

3   Fill bottom halves of pastries with whipped cream and top with fruit. Replace lids and set aside.

4   To make toffee, place sugar and water in a small saucepan. Cook over a medium heat, stirring constantly until sugar dissolves. Continue to cook without stirring until mixture is golden. Remove from heat and stand until bubbles subside. Spin toffee and decorate pastries. Serve within an hour.

Makes 18

Choux pastry is easy to make. Just remember not to tip the flour in before the water mixture is boiling and do not add all the eggs at once.

Miniature Paris Brest

Citrus Meringue Pie

EASY MANGO ICE CREAM

3 mangoes, peeled, seeded and chopped
2 tablespoons lemon juice
³/4 cup/170 g/5¹/2 oz caster sugar
2 eggs, separated
1 cup/250 mL/8 fl oz cream (double)

1   Place mango flesh, lemon juice and sugar in a food processor or blender and process until smooth. Transfer mango mixture to a bowl and refrigerate.

2   Place egg whites in a bowl, beat until stiff peaks form and set aside. Place egg yolks in a separate bowl, beat until thick and creamy and set aside. Place cream in another bowl and whip until soft peaks form. Gently fold whipped cream into egg yolk mixture, then fold in egg whites. Finally, fold the egg mixture into the mango mixture. Spoon into a freezerproof container and freeze until solid.

Serves 4

If you have an ice cream maker, make the ice cream as described in the recipe and freeze in the ice cream maker, following the manufacturer's instructions.

CITRUS MERINGUE PIE

SHORTCRUST PASTRY
2^1/2 cups/315 g/10 oz flour
1 teaspoon caster sugar
220 g/7 oz unsalted butter, chilled and
cut into small squares
^{1}/4-^{1}/2 cup/60-125 mL/2-4 fl oz iced
water

CITRUS FILLING
5 egg yolks
1^1/2 cups/375 mL/12 fl oz sweetened
condensed milk
^{1}/4 cup/60 mL/2 fl oz lemon juice
2 tablespoons lime juice
2 tablespoons orange juice
1 egg white

MERINGUE TOPPING
5 egg whites
^{3}/4 cup/170 g/5^1/2 oz caster sugar

1 To make pastry, place flour, sugar and butter in a food processor and process until mixture resembles fine bread crumbs. With machine running, slowly add iced water until a firm dough forms.

Turn dough onto a lightly floured surface and knead until smooth. Wrap dough in plastic food wrap and refrigerate for 30 minutes.

2 Roll out dough to fit a 20 cm/8 in pie dish. Line pastry case with nonstick baking paper, weigh down with uncooked rice and bake for 10-15 minutes. Remove rice and paper, and cook pastry case for 5-10 minutes longer or until pastry is golden. Set aside to cool.

3 To make filling, place egg yolks, condensed milk, lemon juice, lime juice and orange juice in a bowl and mix to combine. Place egg white in a small bowl and beat until stiff peaks form. Fold egg white into egg yolk mixture and spoon into pastry case.

4 To make topping, place egg whites in a large bowl and beat until frothy. Gradually add sugar, beating well after each addition. Continue beating until stiff peaks form and the mixture is glossy. Cover filling with meringue. Reduce oven temperature to 150°C/300°F/Gas 2. Bake for 10 minutes or until topping is golden.

Serves 6

Oven temperature
200°C, 400°F, Gas 6

For best results when making meringue, beat the egg whites until frothy then slowly beat in the sugar. The secret to a really good meringue is to have as much sugar as possible dissolved on completion of beating.

Easy Mango Ice Cream

LIQUEUR STRAWBERRY SOUFFLE

Oven temperature
180°C, 350°F, Gas 4

Egg whites at room
temperature beat up more
rapidly and have a better
volume than those straight
out of the refrigerator.
Correctly beaten egg whites
will increase by 7-8 times their
original volume.

2 tablespoons Amaretto
(almond liqueur)
2 tablespoons Grand Marnier
(orange liqueur)
250 g/8 oz strawberries, sliced
4 egg yolks
1/3 cup/75 g/2 1/2 oz caster sugar
1/3 cup/45 g/1 1/2 oz flour
1 1/4 cups/315 mL/10 fl oz milk, scalded
1/2 teaspoon vanilla essence
5 egg whites
icing sugar

1   Place Amaretto (almond liqueur),
Grand Marnier (orange liqueur) and
strawberries in a bowl and toss to
combine. Set aside to macerate for
30 minutes.

Serves 6

2   Place egg yolks and sugar in a bowl
and beat until thick and creamy then fold
in flour. Combine milk and vanilla
essence and whisk into egg mixture.
Transfer to a saucepan and heat gently,
stirring constantly, until sauce boils
and thickens. Reduce heat and simmer
for 2 minutes. Set aside to cool slightly.

3   Place egg whites in a bowl and beat
until stiff peaks form. Fold quickly and
lightly into sauce, using a metal spoon.
Place half the strawberries in the base of
a well-greased 20 cm/8 in soufflé dish and
pour over half the soufflé mixture. Repeat
with remaining fruit and mixture.

4   Cook soufflé for 25-30 minutes, or
until well risen and golden brown.
Sprinkle with icing sugar and serve
immediately.

WHITE CHOCOLATE MOUSSE

*This page: White Chocolate Mousse
Opposite page: Liqueur Strawberry
Soufflé*

200 g/6^{1}/$_2$ oz white chocolate
^{1}/$_3$ cup/90 mL/3 fl oz cream (double)
60 g/2 oz butter
3 eggs, separated
75 g/2^{1}/$_2$ oz dark chocolate, melted

1 Place white chocolate and cream in a bowl and place over a saucepan of simmering water. Heat, stirring constantly, until chocolate is melted. Remove bowl from pan and set aside to cool.

2 Beat butter and egg yolks into chocolate mixture, place back over simmering water and cook, stirring constantly, for 2 minutes or until mixture thickens. Remove bowl from pan and set aside.

3 Place egg whites in a bowl and beat until stiff peaks form. Fold egg white mixture into chocolate mixture. Spoon mousse into individual serving glasses and chill for 2 hours.

4 Drizzle melted dark chocolate over each mousse and return to refrigerator until ready to serve.

Serves 4

A rich dessert that would be best served after light first and main courses.

PEARS WITH CHAMPAGNE ZABAGLIONE

This dessert is also delicious served chilled or at room temperature. To serve cold, once the zabaglione is cooked remove bowl from saucepan and place in a sink of iced water. Continue beating until mixture is cold, then refrigerate until ready to use. It is important to beat the mixture while it is cooling down or it will lose its volume and will separate.

4 pears
$^1/_4$ cup/60 mL/2 fl oz lemon juice
$^3/_4$ cup/170 g/5$^1/_2$ oz caster sugar
3 cups/750 mL/1$^1/_4$ pt white wine

CHAMPAGNE ZABAGLIONE
4 egg yolks
$^1/_3$ cup/75 g/2$^1/_2$ oz caster sugar
1 cup/250 mL/8 fl oz champagne or sparkling white wine

Serves 4

1   Peel pears, leaving stalks intact. Place lemon juice, sugar and wine in a saucepan and mix to combine. Add pears, bring to the boil, then reduce heat to simmering and simmer for 25 minutes or until pears are tender.

2   To make zabaglione, place egg yolks and sugar in a bowl and beat to combine. Place bowl over a saucepan of simmering water and cook, beating constantly, until mixture is thick and creamy. Slowly whisk in champagne or wine and continue until mixture is the consistency of a thick custard

3   To serve, remove pears from poaching liquid, place on serving plates and surround with zabaglione. Serve immediately.

CHILLED ZABAGLIONE

Zabaglione is a rich, creamy dessert that makes a delicious finish to any dinner party. You might like to accompany it with a plain dessert biscuit.

6 egg yolks
200 g/6$^1/_2$ oz caster sugar
1 tablespoon finely grated lemon rind
$^1/_4$ cup/60 mL/2 fl oz lemon juice
2 tablespoons Marsala or sweet sherry

1   Place egg yolks, sugar, lemon rind, lemon juice and Marsala or sherry in a bowl and beat until thick and creamy.

2   Place bowl over a saucepan of simmering water and cook, whisking constantly, for 8 minutes or until mixture thickens.

3   Remove bowl from pan and continue beating until mixture cools. Spoon zabaglione into individual serving glasses and chill.

Serves 4

Pears with Champagne Zabaglione,
Chilled Zabaglione

SAUCES

Thick creamy mayonnaise, rich hollandaise and smooth velvety custard all have eggs to thank for their wonderful taste and special textures. Here you will find the best of egg sauces to add that special touch to any meal.

Traditional
Mayonnaise

Egg Sauce

Mornay Sauce

Italian Parsley Sauce

Hollandaise Sauce

Egg Custard

*From top: Traditional
Mayonnaise, Egg Sauce*

TRADITIONAL MAYONNAISE

6 egg yolks
1 teaspoon French mustard
1 tablespoon lemon juice
1 tablespoon tarragon or cider vinegar
1 cup/250 mL/8 fl oz olive oil
1 cup/250 mL/8 fl oz vegetable oil
freshly ground black pepper
1 tablespoon boiling water

1   Place egg yolks, mustard, lemon juice and vinegar in a food processor or blender and process until well mixed. Combine olive and vegetable oils and, with machine running, slowly pour in oil mixture and process until mixture thickens.

2   Season to taste with black pepper and stir in water. Transfer to a jar, cover and refrigerate until required.

Makes 2 cups/500 mL/16 fl oz

Thick, creamy, homemade mayonnaise is easy to make using a food processor, and it adds a touch of indulgence to any salad. If mayonnaise separates, it is because the oil was added too quickly. This is more likely to happen when making mayonnaise by hand than in a food processor. If the mayonnaise separates, place a fresh egg in a clean bowl, whisk lightly and slowly beat in the mayonnaise mixture.

EGG SAUCE

2 hard-boiled eggs
1 tablespoon finely chopped fresh parsley
1 cup/250 mL/8 fl oz milk
30 g/1 oz butter
$^1/_2$ small onion, grated
$^1/_4$ cup/30 g/1 oz flour
1 sprig fresh parsley
2 black peppercorns
pinch ground nutmeg
1 teaspoon lemon juice

1   Cut eggs in half, remove yolks and reserve whites. Rub yolks through a sieve and cut whites into thin strips. Place yolks, whites and parsley in a bowl and mix to combine. Set aside.

2   Place milk in a heavy-based saucepan and warm over a low heat. Melt butter in a separate saucepan and cook onion over a medium heat for 4-5 minutes or until just golden. Stir in flour and cook for 2 minutes.

3   Gradually whisk in milk, then add parsley, peppercorns and nutmeg and cook, stirring constantly, until sauce thickens and boils. Strain sauce through a sieve.

4   Return sauce to a clean saucepan and place over a low heat. Stir in lemon juice, then add egg mixture.

Makes 1$^1/_2$ cups/375 mL/12 fl oz

Traditionally served with steamed or poached fish, this sauce is also delicious spooned over steamed or microwaved vegetables.

MORNAY SAUCE

2 cups/500 mL/16 fl oz milk
60 g/2 oz butter
$^1/_2$ small onion, grated
$^1/_2$ cup/60 g/2 oz flour
1 sprig fresh parsley
4 black peppercorns
$^1/_4$ teaspoon ground nutmeg
3 egg yolks
$^1/_4$ cup/60 mL/2 fl oz cream (double)
30 g/1 oz grated Parmesan cheese

1   Place milk in a heavy-based saucepan and warm over a low heat. Melt butter in a separate saucepan and cook onion over a medium heat for 4-5 minutes or until just golden. Stir in flour and cook for 2 minutes.

2   Gradually whisk in milk, then add parsley, peppercorns and nutmeg and cook, stirring constantly, until sauce thickens and boils. Strain sauce through a sieve and set aside.

3   Place egg yolks and cream in a clean saucepan and whisk to combine. Place pan over a low heat, gradually whisk in sauce and cook, stirring constantly, until sauce comes almost to the boil. Remove pan from heat and stir in cheese.

Makes 2 cups/500 mL/16 fl oz

This sauce is traditionally served hot over steamed fish, chicken and vegetables.

ITALIAN PARSLEY SAUCE

$^1/_2$ cup/30 g/1 oz bread crumbs, made from stale bread
2 tablespoons white wine vinegar
1 hard-boiled egg, yolk only
3 tablespoons finely chopped fresh parsley
2 anchovy fillets, drained and chopped
1 clove garlic, crushed
1 teaspoon finely chopped capers
1 cup/250 mL/8 fl oz olive oil
freshly ground black pepper

1   Place bread crumbs and vinegar in a bowl and set aside to soak.

2   Place egg yolk, parsley, anchovy fillets garlic and capers in a bowl and mash to combine. Squeeze vinegar from bread crumbs and stir bread crumb mixture into egg mixture.

3   Whisk oil into sauce and continue whisking until a smooth, creamy sauce forms. Season to taste with black pepper, cover and set aside to stand for 1-2 hours before using.

Makes 1 cup/250 mL/8 fl oz

This sauce is delicious served with steamed fish or vegetables.

HOLLANDAISE SAUCE

1/4 cup/60 mL/2 fl oz white vinegar
2 tablespoons water
12 black peppercorns
1 bay leaf
3 egg yolks
200 g/6 1/2 oz butter, melted
freshly ground black pepper

1   Place vinegar, water, peppercorns and bay leaf in a saucepan. Bring to the boil and boil until mixture reduces to a third. Remove from heat and set aside to cool.

2   Place egg yolks in a bowl and whisk in 30 g/1 oz butter. Strain vinegar mixture, and whisk into egg mixture. Place bowl over a saucepan of simmering water and whisk mixture constantly until it thickens. Remove saucepan from heat and whisk in remaining butter, a little at a time, until sauce is thick, shiny and resembles a thick cream. Season to taste with black pepper and serve immediately.

Makes 1 cup/250 mL/8 fl oz

The secret to success when making this sauce is to have the temperature right; it should be hot enough to thicken the sauce but not so hot that it will curdle.

EGG CUSTARD

2 cups/500 mL/16 fl oz milk, warmed
5 cm/2 in piece vanilla bean (pod)
3 tablespoons sugar
4 egg yolks

1   Place milk and vanilla bean in a heavy-based saucepan and bring almost to the boil over a low heat. Remove pan from heat and discard vanilla bean.

2   Place sugar and egg yolks in a large bowl and beat until thick and creamy. Whisk in hot milk and place bowl over a saucepan of simmering water. Cook, stirring constantly, until sauce thickens and coats the back of a metal spoon.

Makes 2 cups/500 mL/16 fl oz

This custard can be used as the base for Brandy Sauce or any flavoured custard.
To make a Brandy Sauce, simply stir 2 tablespoons brandy into custard on completion of cooking.
To make a Coffee Liqueur Custard, stir 2 tablespoons strong black coffee and 1 tablespoon coffee liqueur into custard on completion of cooking.

DEVILLED EGGS

12 eggs
2 tablespoons mayonnaise
1 tablespoon cream
1 teaspoon dry mustard
1 teaspoon curry powder
freshly ground black pepper

SUGGESTED GARNISHES

caviar or fish roe; finely chopped spring onions; snipped fresh chives; prawns; olives – stoned and halved; chopped or thinly sliced radish; sliced gherkin; sliced cherry tomatoes; toasted flaked almonds; finely chopped fresh dill; sprigs watercress

2 Remove shells from eggs and cut eggs in half lengthwise. Remove yolks from eggs and reserve egg whites. Push egg yolks through a sieve. Add mayonnaise, cream, mustard and curry powder to egg yolks and mix to combine. Season to taste with black pepper. The mixture should be smooth and of a piping consistency. If it is too thick, mix in a little more cream.

1 Place eggs in a saucepan, pointed end down and packed closely so they stand upright without falling over. Cover with cold water, bring to the boil then reduce heat and simmer for 10 minutes. Drain eggs and run under cold water until cooled.

3 Spoon egg yolk mixture into a piping bag fitted with a small star nozzle and pipe into the reserved egg whites. Garnish as desired.

Makes 24

If preparing these eggs ahead of time, store the yolk mixture in the piping bag and place the whites in a bowl of water. When ready to assemble, drain the whites and fill as described in recipe. If the egg whites will not sit flat, cut a thin slice from the base before filling.

'Always store eggs in the refrigerator. An egg at room temperature loses as much quality and freshness in a day as in 4-5 days in the refrigerator.'

Devilled Eggs

LEMON CURD

1 cup/220 g/7 oz caster sugar
60 g/2 oz butter, chopped into
small pieces
finely grated rind of 2 lemons
juice of 3 lemons
3 eggs, beaten

When making Lemon Curd, care must be taken that the mixture does not boil once the egg yolks are added and that it does not overcook or it will curdle.

1 Place sugar, butter, lemon rind and juice in a bowl and mix to combine.

2 Place bowl over a saucepan of simmering water and cook, stirring frequently, until butter melts.

3 Stir in eggs and cook, stirring constantly, until mixture is thick and creamy. Ladle into hot sterilised jars, seal and set aside to cool. Store in refrigerator for up to 2 weeks.

Makes 2 cups/500 mL/16 fl oz

Lemon Curd

Equipment for Making Omelettes and Crepes

OMELETTE OR CREPE PAN

This should have a thick base so that the omelette will cook rapidly when the pan is heated. The pan can be made of cast iron or aluminium or have a nonstick finish. The base diameter should be 18-19 cm/7-7^1/2 in – which is just the right size for a 2-3 egg omelette – and the side should be outward sloping and about 2.5 cm/1 in high. A 20-23 cm/8-9 in pan is ideal for making larger omelettes of 5-6 eggs.

SEASONING THE PAN

If your pan is made of heavy cast iron or aluminium it will need to be seasoned regularly. All new pans should be seasoned before using. Seasoning the pan creates a smooth surface which prevents the omelette or crêpe mixture from sticking during cooking. To season the pan, sprinkle salt over the surface, heat gently, then rub vigorously with a ball of absorbent kitchen paper. Tip out the excess salt and rub with a clean dry cloth. Alternately the pan can be seasoned with oil. Cover the base of the pan with 1 cm/^{1}/2 in oil and heat over a low heat for 5 minutes, remove pan from heat and set aside for 12 hours. Pour off oil and wipe with absorbent kitchen paper. Follow manufacturer's instructions for seasoning nonstick pans, as if this is done incorrectly the surface can be destroyed.

PAN CARE

A pan used for making omelettes and crêpes should be kept exclusively for this purpose – this ensures that the surface is kept smooth. On completion of cooking, do not wash the pan, simply wipe with absorbent kitchen paper. If the pan starts to stick, do not wash rather, repeat one of the seasoning processes as described.

THE PERFECT OMELETTE

There are many different omelettes, but the one that seems to hold the greatest mystery is the traditional 2-egg, meal-in-a-jiffy, plain French omelette. Once you have mastered it, you will wonder what all the fuss was about.

PREPARING THE OMELETTE

Place the eggs, water and seasonings in a bowl and lightly whisk to combine. Allow 1 teaspoon of cold water for each egg used – this makes for a light omelette.

THE COOKED OMELETTE

This should be only lightly set, with the top still moist. Once cooked, fold over one-third of the omelette away from the handle of pan. Hold pan over a warm serving plate, with the palm of your hand uppermost. Shake omelette to edge of pan and tip to make another fold and slip onto serving plate. If preferred, the omelette can be folded in half. The cooked omelette can be sprinkled with a filling before folding. Always serve an omelette immediately it is cooked.

COOKING THE OMELETTE

Start by melting a knob of butter in the pan over a medium heat and tilt the pan to ensure that the entire surface is covered. When melted, the butter will foam and then subside. This is the time to pour in the eggs. Wait a few seconds to allow a thin film of egg to form on the bottom of the pan and, using a fork, gently draw in the sides of the omelette, allowing the uncooked liquid to flow onto the pan surface. Continue in this way until the omelette is cooked.

The best omelettes are made with 2 or 3 eggs for a single serve. As the cooking time is short, the omelette will not overcook and toughen.

BEAN SPROUT OMELETTE

1 teaspoon butter
2 eggs
2 teaspoons water
freshly ground black pepper

BEAN SPROUT FILLING
30 g/1 oz butter
2 teaspoons grated fresh ginger
4 tablespoons bean sprouts
1 tablespoon snipped fresh chives

1   To make filling, melt butter in a small frying pan and cook ginger, bean sprouts and chives for 1 minute. Remove pan from heat and keep warm.

2   Melt butter in a small omelette pan. Lightly whisk together eggs, water and black pepper to taste. Pour into heated pan and cook over a medium heat. Continually draw edge of omelette in with a fork during cooking until no liquid remains and omelette is lightly set.

3   Sprinkle the bean sprout mixture over omelette and fold. Slip onto a plate and serve immediately.

Serves 1

Bean Sprout Omelette

RATATOUILLE CREPES

Oven temperature
180°C, 350°F, Gas 4

To keep cooked crêpes warm while making the rest of the batch, place the crêpes in a stack on a heatproof plate and place in a low oven, or over a saucepan of simmering water.

To freeze crêpes, stack cold crêpes between sheets of greaseproof paper or freezer wrap and place in a sealed freezer bag, or wrap tightly in aluminium foil. To use crêpes, thaw at room temperature, then fill and reheat. To use directly from frozen, remove greaseproof or freezer wrap, stack 4-6 crêpes, wrap in foil and heat in oven at 200°C/400°F/Gas 6 for 25 minutes.

$^1/_2$ cup/30 g/1 oz **bread crumbs, made from stale bread**
125 g/4 oz **grated tasty cheese (mature Cheddar)**

CREPES
1 cup/125 g/4 oz **flour, sifted**
2 **eggs**
$1^1/_4$ cups/315 mL/10 fl oz **milk**
15 g/$^1/_2$ oz **butter, melted**

RATATOUILLE FILLING
1 **eggplant (aubergine), cut into 2 cm/$^3/_4$ in cubes**
2 tablespoons **olive oil**
1 **onion, chopped**
440 g/14 oz **canned tomatoes, undrained and mashed**
1 teaspoon **dried oregano**

1   To make crêpes, place flour in a bowl and make a well in the centre. Add eggs and a little milk and beat, working in all the flour. Beat in butter and remaining milk.

2   Pour 2-3 tablespoons batter into a lightly greased 18 cm/7 in crêpe pan and tilt pan so batter covers base thinly and evenly. Cook over a high heat for 1 minute or until lightly browned on base.

3   Turn crêpe, using a palette knife, and cook second side for 30 seconds. Remove from pan and set aside. Repeat with remaining mixture.

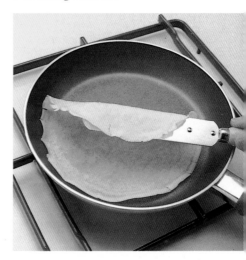

4   To make filling, place eggplant (aubergine) in a colander, set over a bowl, sprinkle with salt and allow to stand for 30 minutes. Rinse under cold water and pat dry with absorbent kitchen paper. Heat oil in a large frying pan and cook onion over a medium heat for 4-5 minutes or until soft. Add eggplant (aubergine), tomatoes and oregano and bring to the boil, then reduce heat and simmer, uncovered, for 15-20 minutes or until mixture reduces and thickens. Remove pan from heat and set aside to cool.

5   Divide filling between crêpes and roll up. Place crêpes in a single layer in a shallow ovenproof dish. Place bread crumbs and cheese in a bowl, mix to combine, sprinkle over crêpes and bake for 30 minutes.

Serves 4

Ratatouille Crêpes

SERVING AND PRESENTING CREPES

For interest and variety, vary the ways in which you serve crêpes. A stack is great when feeding a crowd, while individual parcels can hold surprise fillings.

One of the simplest ways to serve crêpes is flat, topped with interesting ingredients. One of the most popular ways to serve them is to spread the filling over the crêpe then roll it.

To make individual parcels, place the filling in the centre of the crêpe, fold in the sides and gently roll up.

Crêpe cones are easy to make and they are a fun way of serving crêpes. To make a cone, fold the crêpe in half, then in half again to make a triangular shape. Open the top and spoon the filling into the pocket.

To make a crêpe stack, place one crêpe on a serving plate, spread with filling, then top with a second crêpe. Continue in this way until the stack is as high as you want it. Serve stacks cut into wedges.

OMELETTE SHREDS

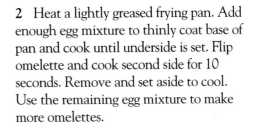

3 eggs
1 tablespoon cold water
freshly ground black pepper
1 tablespoon finely chopped fresh herbs,
such as parsley, chives or coriander
(optional)

2   Heat a lightly greased frying pan. Add enough egg mixture to thinly coat base of pan and cook until underside is set. Flip omelette and cook second side for 10 seconds. Remove and set aside to cool. Use the remaining egg mixture to make more omelettes.

One of the classic Asian garnishes, Omelette Shreds are quick and easy to make when you know how. Use as a garnish for soups, fried rice and noodle dishes and in salads.

1   Place eggs, water, black pepper to taste and herbs, if using, in a bowl and whisk to combine.

3   To make shreds, place cold omelettes in a stack, roll up and cut into fine shreds.

The omelettes can also be cut into 2.5 cm/1 in squares.

Omelette Shreds

COOKING THE PERFECT EGG

Many of the simplest dishes are in fact the most difficult to cook perfectly – this is particularly true of eggs. Use these pointers to cook a perfect egg every time.

HARD-BOILED EGGS

Quick cooling of hard-boiled eggs prevents a dark ring forming around the yolk.

eggs at room temperature

1   Tightly pack eggs into a saucepan, pointed end down, cover with water and bring to the boil. Boil for 10 minutes. Drain eggs and cool under cold running water.

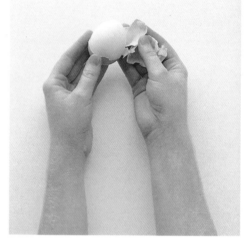

2   Peel eggs as soon as they are cool. Use as desired.

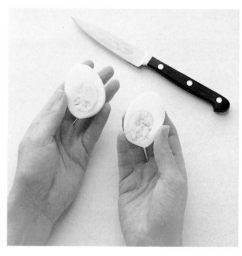

This technique for boiling eggs ensures that the yolk is centred, so it is a good technique to use for stuffed eggs and the like.

SOFT-BOILED EGGS

Bring a saucepan of water to the boil, reduce heat to simmering and add eggs. Cook for 3 minutes for a light set and $4^1/2$ minutes for a slightly firmer set.

POACHED EGGS

Bring a frying pan of water to simmering. Break egg into a cup and slide into simmering water. Cook for 3-4 minutes or until egg is cooked to your liking.

FRIED EGGS

Heat a little oil or melt a knob of butter in a frying pan. Break egg into a cup and slide into pan. Cook over a medium heat until white is set and the yolk still runny. This is what is often called 'sunny side up'. Some people like to flip their eggs to cook the top and in so doing make a 'right side over easy'.

MICROWAVING EGGS

POACHED EGG: One-quarter fill a cup or small ramekin with hot water and heat on HIGH (100%) for 30 seconds or until boiling. Add egg, pierce the yolk several times using the tip of a sharp knife or a skewer and cook on MEDIUM-HIGH (70%) for 45 seconds-1 minute or until egg is cooked to your liking.

BAKED EGG: Place egg in a lightly greased cup or ramekin Pierce yolk several times using the tip of a sharp knife or a skewer and cook on MEDIUM (50%) for 1-$1^1/2$ minutes or until egg is cooked to your liking.

FRIED EGGS: To fry eggs in the microwave you will need a browning dish. Preheat browning dish according to the manufacturer's instructions – heat the dish for the longest recommended time – add a knob of butter and swirl to coat the dish. Break 2 eggs into dish, pierce yolks several times using the tip of a sharp knife or a skewer and cook on MEDIUM-HIGH (70%) for 30-45 seconds or until eggs are cooked to your liking.

SCRAMBLED EGGS: Scrambled eggs cook well in the microwave. Melt 15 g/$^1/2$ oz butter in a microwave-safe jug or dish, add 2 eggs, 2 tablespoons milk and black pepper to taste and cook on MEDIUM (50%) for $1^1/2$-2 minutes or until egg mixture is set but still creamy. Stir twice during cooking.

BOILED EGGS: Unless you have a special microwave egg boiler it is not recommended that you boil eggs in the microwave as they can explode, causing damage to your microwave.

Scrambled eggs are one of the foods that you can cook most successfully in the microwave.

'A quick way to test if an egg in its shell is fresh is to place it in a glass of water. If it is fresh it will sink straight to the bottom, while a bad egg will float. If the egg stands on its end it is a week or more old.'

TYPES OF EGGS

While there are many different types of eggs used in cooking – quail, goose, duck, seagull, ostrich, pheasant, to name but a few – it is the egg of the domestic hen which is most often used and it is this egg we think of when talking about eggs.

Did you know?
An average-sized ostrich egg weighs 1.5 kg/3 lb and takes 40 minutes to boil.
The largest eggs were laid by the now extinct elephant bird. The eggs of this bird weighed about 12 kg/24 lb.

QUAILS' EGGS
These are about one-third the size of a hen's egg and have a pretty greenish-beige shell with dark spots. Popular as a gourmet item, they are usually available from specialty food and poultry shops.

FREE-RANGE EGGS
In recent years there has been much concern about battery-raised chickens and the eggs from them. Free-range eggs have become popular, however it should be noted that, while the breeding of free-range chickens may be considered to be more humane, the actual nutritional value of the eggs is not greatly different from that of eggs from battery-raised chickens. Due to the space required to raise free-range chickens these eggs are more expensive, nevertheless most people believe that the flavour is well worth the extra expense.

POLYUNSATURATED EGGS
These contain a greater proportion of polyunsaturated fat, but their cholesterol count is similar to ordinary eggs. The chickens are reared on a special feed rich in polyunsaturated seeds, blended with soyameal, sunflower seeds and grains, which alters the composition of the eggs they lay.

EGG SUBSTITUTE
This is a useful product for those on low-cholesterol diets and, while it cannot create a whole poached or boiled egg, it can be used to make omelettes, scrambled eggs, pancakes and in general cooking. It is made from egg whites, skim milk powder, polyunsaturated vegetable oil, emulsifier and beta-carotene (the source of the yellow-orange colour of carrots and many other vegetables). Its cholesterol is only a fraction of that of eggs, and its fat is high in polyunsaturates.

What's in an Egg?

An egg weighing 60 g/2 oz with its shell on supplies you with approximately 6 g protein, 6 g fat, a trace of sugars and starch, no dietary fibre and 355 kJ/ 85 Calories.

About 75% of an egg is water, 12% is protein and 12% is fat. Eggs also contain good amounts of calcium, phosphorus, potassium, zinc and iron – however it should be remembered that the iron in eggs is not well absorbed by humans. Eggs are also good sources of the B group vitamins, plus vitamins A, D and E. In fact the only nutrients not present in eggs are vitamin C and fibre.

In recent years there has been much publicity about the amount of cholesterol contained in eggs and while one egg contains about 250 mg cholesterol, (National Heart Foundation's recommended maximum daily allowance for cholesterol is 300 mg) this should not stop you from including them as part of a balanced diet. Those who should be most concerned about eating eggs are those with high blood cholesterol. If you fall into this group it is advised that you should limit your egg intake to two per week.

Buying and Storing Eggs

Always buy eggs from a reliable source with a high turnover to ensure you are getting the freshest possible eggs. In some countries in recent years there has been concern over the levels of salmonella bacteria in eggs. Any risks can be eliminated by making sure that eggs are well cooked. When making mayonnaise, adding vinegar to the yolk first will kill any bacteria. In meringues and icings the high proportion of sugar prevents problems.

Eggs should be stored in the refrigerator with the pointed end down – this helps keep the yolk centred. There is no need to remove the eggs from their carton for storage; keeping the eggs in their carton in fact protects them from odours. The shell of an egg is porous, so if stored with strong-smelling foods, such as onions, the eggs can absorb and take on that flavour. On storage, eggs start to dehydrate. This process happens more quickly if the eggs are stored at room temperature and if they are left uncovered during storage.

LEFTOVER EGGS: Keep leftover yolks and whites in an airtight container in the refrigerator. Place 1 tablespoon of water over the yolks to prevent a skin forming. Yolks will keep for up to 3 days and whites for up to 10 days. You can freeze whites for up to a month.

USEFUL INFORMATION

Can sizes vary between countries and manufacturers. You may find the quantities in this book are slightly different from what is available. Purchase and use the can size nearest to the suggested size in the recipe.

In this book, ingredients such as fish and meat are given in grams so you know how much to buy. It is handy to have:
- A small inexpensive set of kitchen scales.

Other ingredients in our recipes are given in tablespoons and cups, so you will need:
- A nest of measuring cups (1 cup, $^1/2$ cup, $^1/3$ cup and $^1/4$ cup).
- A set of measuring spoons (1 tablespoon, 1 teaspoon, $^1/2$ teaspoon and $^1/4$ teaspoon).
- A transparent graduated measuring jug (1 litre or 250 mL) for measuring liquids.
- Cup and spoon measures are level.

QUICK CONVERTER

Metric	Imperial
5 mm	$^1/4$ in
1 cm	$^1/2$ in
2 cm	$^3/4$ in
2.5 cm	1 in
5 cm	2 in
10 cm	4 in
15 cm	6 in
20 cm	8 in
23 cm	9 in
25 cm	10 in
30 cm	12 in

MEASURING LIQUIDS

Metric	Imperial	Cup
30 mL	1 fl oz	
60 mL	2 fl oz	$^1/4$ cup
90 mL	3 fl oz	
125 mL	4 fl oz	$^1/2$ cup
155 mL	5 fl oz	
170 mL	$5^1/2$ fl oz	$^2/3$ cup
185 mL	6 fl oz	
220 mL	7 fl oz	
250 mL	8 fl oz	1 cup
500 mL	16 fl oz	2 cups
600 mL	20 fl oz (1 pt)	
750 mL	$1^1/4$ pt	
1 litre	$1^3/4$ pt	4 cups
1.2 litres	2 pt	

METRIC CUPS & SPOONS

Metric	Cups	Imperial
60 mL	$^1/4$ cup	2 fl oz
80 mL	$^1/3$ cup	$2^1/2$ fl oz
125 mL	$^1/2$ cup	4 fl oz
250 mL	1 cup	8 fl oz
	Spoons	
1.25 mL	$^1/4$ teaspoon	
2.5 mL	$^1/2$ teaspoon	
5 mL	1 teaspoon	
20 mL	1 tablespoon	

MEASURING DRY INGREDIENTS

Metric	Imperial
15 g	$^1/2$ oz
30 g	1 oz
60 g	2 oz
90 g	3 oz
125 g	4 oz
155 g	5 oz
185 g	6 oz
220 g	7 oz
250 g	8 oz
280 g	9 oz
315 g	10 oz
375 g	12 oz
410 g	13 oz
440 g	14 oz
470 g	15 oz
500 g	16 oz (1 lb)
750 g	1 lb 8 oz
1 kg	2 lb
1.5 kg	3 lb

OVEN TEMPERATURES

°C	°F	Gas Mark
120	250	$^1/2$
140	275	1
150	300	2
160	325	3
180	350	4
190	375	5
200	400	6
220	425	7
240	475	8
250	500	9

INDEX

UK COOKERY EDITOR
Katie Swallow

EDITORIAL
Food Editor: Rachel Blackmore
Editorial Assistant: Ella Martin
Editorial Co-ordinator: Margaret Kelly
Recipe Development: Sheryle Eastwood, Lucy Kelly, Donna Hay,
Voula Maritzouridis, Anneka Mitchell, Penelope Peel, Belinda Warn,
Loukie Werle
Credits: Recipes pages 62, 63 Gordon Grimsdale; page 66 by Mary
Norwak; page 73 June Budgen © Merehurst Limited

COVER
Photography: Ashley Mackevicius
Styling: Wendy Berecry

PHOTOGRAPHY
Per Ericson, Ashley Mackevicius, Harm Mol, Yanto Noerianto,
Andy Payne, Jon Stewart, Warren Webb

STYLING
Wendy Berecry, Belinda Clayton, Rosemary De Santis, Carolyn
Fienberg, Jacqui Hing, Michelle Gorry

DESIGN AND PRODUCTION
Manager: Sheridan Carter
Layout and Finished Art: Lulu Dougherty
Design: Frank Pithers

Published by J.B. Fairfax Press Pty Limited
A.C.N. 003 738 430
Formatted by J.B. Fairfax Press Pty Limited
Printed by Toppan Printing Co, Singapore

© J.B. Fairfax Press Pty Limited, 1992
This book is copyright. No part may be reproduced or transmitted
without the written permission of the publisher. Enquiries should be
made in writing to the publisher.

JBFP 178 UK
Includes Index
ISBN 1 86343 052 0 (pbk)
ISBN 1 85391 284 0

Distributed by J.B. Fairfax Press Ltd
9 Trinity Centre, Park Farm Estate
Wellingborough, Northants, UK
Ph: (0933) 402330 Fax: (0933) 402234